100 great recipes

Potato

100 great recipes

Potato

Jacqueline Bellefontaine

Published by SILVERDALE BOOKS
An imprint of Bookmart Ltd
Registered number 2372865
Trading as Bookmart Ltd
Blaby Road
Wigston
Leicester LE18 4SE

©2005 D&S Books Ltd

D&S Books Ltd
Kerswell,
Parkham Ash, Bideford
Devon, England
EX39 5PR

e-mail us at:- enquiries@d-sbooks.co.uk

This edition printed 2005

ISBN 1-84509-177-9

DS0100. 100 Great Potato Recipes

Creative Director: Sarah King
Editor: Sally MacEachern
Project editor: Anna Southgate
Designer: Debbie Fisher
Photographer: Colin Bowling/Paul Forrester

Fonts: New York, Helvetica and Bradley Hand

Printed in China

1 3 5 7 9 10 8 6 4 2

Contents

introduction

The importance and appeal of the potato have varied over the centuries but their popularity is once more on the increase in many parts of the world. In fact, restaurants in London and New York have made the spud truly fashionable again, with mash in its many guises appearing on even the most expensive menus.

The humble potato is the most important vegetable in the world and the fourth most important staple food after rice, wheat and corn. It is cultivated in most countries, with Russia, Poland and Germany the biggest consumers, closely followed by Holland, Cyprus and Ireland. The average person eats 109kg/242lb of potatoes per head a year. The potato has a high nutritional value and is low in fat and calories, making it ideal for those who want to follow a healthy diet.

The potato is a very versatile vegetable that can be cooked in a multitude of ways. It complements numerous other flavours, making it ideal for everyday cooking, as well as special occasions. Potatoes are quick and easy to prepare, inexpensive and loved by children and adults alike, making them a real family favourite.

I have brought together an array of classic and contemporary recipes from around the globe, ranging from soups to salads, and from family meals to side dishes. The recipes will inspire you to use potatoes in both traditional and imaginative new ways. The botanically unrelated, but equally important, sweet potato has not been forgotten and recipes for this delicious vegetable are also included.

This book really is a tribute to the versatility of this most humble of vegetables.

The history of the potato

The potato originates from South America; there is evidence of its cultivation in Peru as early as 3000BC. The potato was brought to Europe by Spanish explorers towards the end of the 16th century. Cultivation spread slowly from Spain to Italy, then Belgium and Germany. By the beginning of the 17th century, the potato was widely grown in Ireland and it was the Irish who took the potato to North America in the early 18th century. Here it became known as the Irish potato in order to distinguish it from the unrelated sweet potato. England and Scotland started to cultivate the potato widely as late as the 19th century and were followed by France.

The Irish potato famine in the 19th century was caused by a fungal disease that destroyed almost the entire potato crop, not just once but three times. As the country's staple food was wiped out, over one million people died and many more emigrated to England and the United States.

During the Second World War supplies of American and Canadian wheat dwindled and the potato played an important part in the British diet.

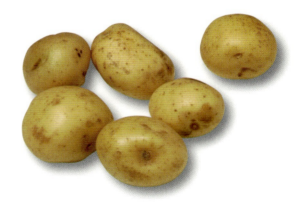

Today, the potato's use as foods such as mash and frozen chips, combined with its low cost, make the food as popular now as it has been at any time.

The healthy potato

Potatoes have a high nutritional value. They are an important source of vitamin C – one medium 175g/6oz portion of new potatoes provides 26% of the Recommended Daily Allowance (RDA). They are an important source of B vitamins, providing 30% RDA of B6. Potatoes are rich in potassium and iron and, if served in the skins, an important source of fibre. In fact, one medium baked potato has the same amount of fibre as two slices of wholemeal bread. Most of the minerals and vitamins in potatoes are just under the skin so it is a good idea to serve them regularly in their skins. This is great news for those who prefer to leave the potato peeler in the drawer. Cooking potatoes in their skins prevents nutrients from leaching out into the water; so even if you prefer to eat them without skins, consider boiling them in their skins and peeling them once cooked. Always wash potatoes before use. Potato water can be used as a base for stock and in soups.

For the weight-conscious among us, it is good to know that the potato is low in fat and contains no cholesterol. A 225g/8oz serving of boiled potatoes averages 16 calories. However, putting butter on potatoes or frying them can bump up the calories considerably, so consider this when choosing potato recipes if you want to keep the calories low. Independent nutritionist and dietary researchers recommend potatoes as the perfect base for a balanced meal.

The well-kept potato

When buying potatoes look for firm, smooth skin that is not wrinkled, withered or cracked. Avoid potatoes that are sprouting or turning green.

To store, remove from the plastic bag. Potatoes are best stored in a paper or cloth bag. Store away from onions and other strong-smelling ingredients in a cool, dark and airy place – not the refrigerator.

The seasonal potato

Potatoes are generally classified according to their growing season. Potatoes taken out of the ground earlier in the season are called earlies or new potatoes. Those harvested later are called main crop potatoes.

In Europe, new potatoes are harvested as early as mid-April and are in the shops from May to July. Main crop potatoes are planted in April and harvested from September to October; they store well and are available all year round, although different varieties are available at different times.

Second earlies are harvested and available between the two main seasons.

The versatile potato

There are over 400 varieties of potato but sadly only around 30 are grown commercially in any quantity. Nonetheless, new varieties are beginning to appear, most notably in the speciality and salad varieties. Each variety has its own characteristics and each is suited to different cooking methods. Some are suitable for just one type of cooking, while others are more adaptable and make good all-rounders. In general, however, they can be divided into two main types: floury potatoes, which have a more granular, drier, fluffier texture and are perfect for mash, chips, baked potatoes and fluffy roast potatoes; and waxy potatoes, which have translucent, moist flesh and stay firm when cooked, are ideal for boiling.

A new class of potato, which is beginning to make an appearance, is the speciality or salad potato. These are firm potatoes, generally waxy in texture, that are ideal for boiling and have their own distinct flavour.

A selection of potato varieties and their uses

Whether you classify potatoes as new and main crop or as floury and waxy, they will still have anomalies. Some waxy potatoes are suitable for cooking methods generally thought to be more suited to floury potatoes and vice versa. For the recipes in this book I have specified new, waxy or floury potatoes when necessary. However, with some recipes both floury and waxy potatoes produce good results, in which case I have not specified a type. Most supermarket packaging specifies the suitability of the potato variety to the various methods of cooking.

Floury potatoes

Name	Characteristics	Good for
Desiree	Firm, slightly waxy texture; oval shape; red skin and light yellow flesh	Boiling, baking, roasting, chips and mash
Maris Piper	Floury texture; short, oval shape; cream skin and flesh	Baking, chips, roasting and mash
King Edward	Soft, floury texture; long, oval shape; white skin with pink coloration and cream flesh	Baking, chips, roasting and mash
Romano	Soft, dry texture; short, oval shape; red skin and cream flesh	Boiling, baking roasting and mash

Maris Piper

Desiree

Jersey Royal

Nicola

Carlingford

Sante

Waxy Potatoes

Name	Characteristics	Good for
Cara	Firm, moist texture; short to oval shape; white skin with pink eyes and cream flesh	Boiling and chips
Carlingford	White skin and flesh; firm texture	Boiling
Estima	Firm, moist texture; oval shape; light skin and light yellow flesh	Boiling and baking
Maris Bard	White skin and pale cream flesh	Boiling
Maris peer	Cream skin and flesh; firm cooked texture	Boiling, chips
Marfona	Firm, moist texture; short, oval shape; light yellow skin and light yellow flesh	Boiling and baking
Nadine	Firm, waxy texture; oval shape; cream skin and flesh	Boiling and roasting
Sante	Dry, firm texture; short, oval shape; light yellow skin and light yellow flesh	Boiling, roasting and chips
Wilja	Moderately firm, waxy texture; long, oval shape; yellow skin and light yellow flesh	Boiling, roasting, chips and mash

Salad/Speciality Potatoes

Name	Characteristics	Good for
Black Potatoes	Colour changes to dark purple when cooked	Novelty value
Charlotte	Firm, waxy texture; oval to long shape; light yellow skin and yellow flesh	Boiling, salads
Jersey Royals	Flaky skin and firm, yellow flesh; limited season	Boiling, salads
La Ratte, also known as Belle de Fontenay	French potato with smooth, yellow skin, long shape and yellow flesh	Boiling, salads
Nicola	Firm cooked texture; long, oval shape; yellow skin and light yellow flesh	Boiling, salads
Pink Fir Apple	Long, knobbly, finger-shaped, pinkish skin with yellow flesh	Boiling, salads

Black Potato

La Ratte

Pink Fir Apple

The well-cooked potato

Potatoes can be cooked in many ways: whole, cut into chunks, grated or sliced. They can be boiled, baked or fried – the options are almost endless. To preserve their nutritional content, potatoes are best cooked in their skins but whether or not you do this is a matter of preference.

Boiled Potatoes

Choose potatoes of a similar size to ensure even cooking or cut into equal size pieces. New potatoes are best cooked unpeeled. Simply wash well and scrape away any flaky skin with a sharp knife if desired. Add to lightly salted boiling water. Main crop potatoes can be boiled in their skins or peeled. Potatoes cooked in their skins retain more nutrients and absorb less water. If you prefer peeled potatoes but want to maintain the maximum nutrients then peel after cooking. Allow to cool slightly and hold in a clean cloth. Cooking times will vary depending on the size of the potatoes or potato pieces. As a guide, baby new potatoes may take as little as 12 minutes, small potatoes about 15–20 minutes, large potatoes quartered about 20 minutes or whole large potatoes up to 40 minutes. Always cover the pan to help reduce the cooking time.

To test if cooked:
I like to use a metal skewer to test potatoes, but a sharp knife can also be used. Test for tenderness towards the end of the expected cooking time or the potatoes may start to absorb water and break up before they are cooked, through.

Steamed Potatoes

Steaming potatoes takes a little longer than boiling but will retain more nutrients, as vitamins are not leached out into the cooking water. It is an ideal way of cooking small whole potatoes.

Mashed Potato

Choose a floury potato. Consider cooking potatoes in their skins before peeling and mashing. This produces a drier potato which will better take up additional flavourings and liquids. If peeling and cutting into chunks, make sure all the chunks are of an equal size. Once cooked, drain well and return to the heat for a few seconds to drive off any remaining moisture. Use a potato masher, potato ricer (like a giant garlic press) or an electric whisk to mash the potatoes and always warm liquids before adding to mash.

Baked Potatoes

Baked potatoes can be served as an accompaniment to a meal or served as a meal in itself topped with a few flavourings such as cheese or tuna. Choose equal sized potatoes and scrub well. Prick all over with a fork to allow steam to escape and to prevent the potato bursting during cooking. Cook at 200°C/400°F/gas mark 6 for 1 to 1¹/₂ hours until tender.

A quick and convenient way to bake a potato especially if only for 1 or 2 people is in the microwave, but you will not get the lovely crisp skin of a conventionally baked spud. Prick all over with a fork and cook on high. One potato will take 8–10 minutes, two about 15 minutes. Four about 20–25 minutes. Allow to stand for 5 minutes before serving.

Roast Potatoes

Choose floury potatoes for a traditional roast with a crisp surface and fluffy inside. Potatoes can be roasted peeled or in their skins. Again it is important to choose potatoes of a similar size or cut into equal size pieces to ensure even cooking. Peeled potatoes can be par-boiled first, by placing in a pan of boiling water, quickly returning to the boil and cooking for 4–5 minutes. Drain and return to the pan. Place the lid on the pan and shake a few times to roughen up the surface of the potato, this will produce a roast potato with a really crisp surface. Goose fat, duck fat, dripping or lard will all add extra flavour to the potatoes but are high in saturated fat. Olive oil, sunflower, ground nut or a blended vegetable oil can be used, and do not contain saturated fats.

Heat the fat or oil in the oven before adding the potatoes. The oven temperature should be high 200°C/400°F/gas mark 6 or 220°C/425°F/gas mark 7. Turn to coat in the oil once or twice during the cooking time which will be about 1 hour. Roast potatoes can be cooked in the pan around the joint of meat, but here they tend to absorb the meat juices which, whilst having flavour, can make the potatoes soggy, so I prefer to cook them above the meat on a separate tray. Small, new, waxy potatoes can also be roasted in their skins, they have a different texture and are delicious used in salads or served hot tossed in a flavoured dressing.

Oven Chips and Wedges

Cut potatoes into wedges or chips with or without peeling, toss in a little oil and roast for 20–25 minutes at 200°C/400°F/gas mark 6, for a low-fat alternative to the fried chip.

Deep-fried Potatoes

The key to successful deep-frying is the oil temperature which should be 180–190°C (350–375°F). If the oil is too cool, the chips will absorb the fat and be soggy. If it is too high the chips will burn on the outside and may be uncooked inside. Make sure the potatoes are dry before adding to the fat and lower slowly into the oil to prevent splashing. Do not overcrowd the pan or the oil temperature will drop too much and the chips will not brown. Never leave a chip pan unattended . If you fry regularly it is a good idea to invest in a deep-fat fryer for both convenience and safety. Drain the potatoes on absorbent kitchen paper after frying to remove the excess oil.

Shallow-fried Potatoes

Shallow-frying is a great way to use up leftover potato. Slice or cut the potatoes into small chunks. Use a heavy based pan – a sauté pan if you have one, which makes turning the potatoes over as they cook easier.

Tips for Successful Cooking

- Use metric or imperial measurements only; do not mix the two.

- Use measuring spoons: 1 tsp = 5ml; 1tbsp = 15ml

- All spoon measurements are level unless otherwise stated.

- All eggs are medium unless otherwise stated.

- Recipes using raw or lightly cooked eggs should not be given to babies, pregnant woman, the very old or anyone suffering from or recovering from an illness.

- The cooking times are an approximate guide only. If you are using a fan oven reduce the cooking time according to the manufacturers instructions.

- Ovens should be preheated to the required temperature.

- Fruits and vegetables should be washed before use.

Please note – most of the recipes have ingredients listed for a number of servings. If the recipe includes servings for two and four people, for example, the recipe will show how much to add for two people, with amount for four people in brackets. ie.: '2 tbspns (4 tblspns)'.

soups *and*
starters

Cream of Cauliflower Soup

Potatoes are often used in soups as a thickening agent. Here they combine with the subtle flavour of cauliflower in a delicious creamy soup.

Ingredients for 2

25g/1oz butter
2 shallots, chopped
1/2 small cauliflower (about 225g/8oz), trimmed and roughly chopped
175g/6oz floury potatoes, peeled & cut into chunks
300ml/1/2pt vegetable stock
150ml/1/4pt milk
salt and freshly ground black pepper
a little grated nutmeg
75ml/2 1/2fl oz single or double cream
chopped parsley, to garnish

Ingredients for 4

50g/2oz butter
4 shallots, chopped
1 small cauliflower (about 450g/1lb), trimmed and roughly chopped
350g/12oz floury potatoes, peeled & cut into chunks
600ml/1pt vegetable stock
300ml/1/2pt milk
salt and freshly ground black pepper
a little grated nutmeg
150ml/1/4pt single or double cream
chopped parsley, to garnish

1 Melt the butter in a saucepan and sauté shallots until softened.

2 Add the cauliflower and potatoes to the pan and cook gently for 5 minutes.

3 Add stock and milk and bring to the boil. Reduce the heat and simmer gently for 30 minutes.

4 Season with salt, pepper and a generous pinch of freshly grated nutmeg.

5 Purée the soup in a liquidizer or food processor and return to the pan.

6 Stir in the single cream and reheat. Do not let it return to the boil at this point. Serve garnished with a sprinkling of chopped parsley.

Vichyssoise

Easy Entertaining

This classic dish is traditionally served cold and has a delicate flavour. It should be passed through a sieve after puréeing to ensure a really smooth texture. If you do not like chilled soups (my children will not even try them), you can serve it warm, when it becomes the less glamorous sounding, but nonetheless delicious, leek and potato soup. In this case, you can omit passing the soup through a sieve as a rougher texture is fine for a hot soup.

Ingredients for 2

2 large leeks
25g/1oz butter
1 shallot, chopped
225g/8oz floury potatoes,
    peeled and diced
375ml/13fl oz good chicken
    or vegetable stock
1 bay leaf
2 sprigs parsley
75ml/2¹/₂fl oz double cream
salt and white pepper
fresh chives to garnish

Ingredients for 4

4 large leeks
50g/2oz butter
2 shallots, chopped
450g/1lb floury potatoes,
    peeled and diced
750ml/1¹/₄pt good chicken or
    vegetable stock
1 bay leaf
2 sprigs parsley
150ml/¹/₄pt double cream
salt and white pepper
fresh chives, to garnish

1 Trim the leeks and discard the green parts. Slit the leeks lengthwise and wash out the dirt. Shake them dry and then chop finely.

2 Melt the butter in a saucepan and gently sauté the shallots for a few minutes until softened.

3 Stir in the leeks and potatoes and cook gently, stirring frequently, for 10 minutes.

4 Add the stock and herbs and bring to the boil. Reduce the heat, cover and simmer for 30 minutes. Stir in the cream.

5 Allow to cool slightly and then purée in a liquidizer. Strain through a sieve. Allow to cool completely and then chill until required.

6 Check the seasoning and add a little salt and white pepper if required. Serve garnished with fresh chives.

Curried Potato Soup

Low Fat

You can have this soup cooked and ready to eat in about 30 minutes, making it a great midweek meal. I like to serve it with naan bread and coriander chutney.

Ingredients for 2

1 tbsp sunflower oil
1 small onion, chopped
1 clove garlic, chopped
150g/5oz floury potatoes,
   peeled and diced
1–2 tsp medium or mild
   curry paste
450ml/³/4pt vegetable stock
50g/2oz frozen peas
25g/1oz small spinach leaves
3 tbsp natural yoghurt

Ingredients for 4

2 tbsp sunflower oil
1 large onion, chopped
2 cloves garlic, chopped
275g/10oz floury potatoes,
   peeled and diced
1 tbsp medium or mild
   curry paste
900ml/1¹/2pt vegetable stock
100g/4oz frozen peas
50g/2oz small spinach leaves
6 tbsp natural yoghurt

1 Heat the oil in a large saucepan and fry the onion for 3–4 minutes until beginning to soften.

2 Add the garlic and potatoes and fry gently, stirring constantly, for 5 minutes.

3 Stir in the curry paste and cook for 1 minute, stirring.

4 Stir in the stock and bring to the boil. Reduce the heat, cover and simmer for about 15 minutes until the potato begins to break up.

5 Add the peas and spinach and cook for a further 5 minutes.

6 Remove from the heat and stir in the natural yoghurt. Serve immediately.

Potato Soup with Roasted Garlic and Parsley

This has to be one of the tastiest soups I make and yet it is made from the most humble of ingredients. This recipe gives a mildly garlic flavour but if you are a garlic fan feel free to increase the amount of garlic. There is no need to peel the garlic before roasting, just squeeze it out of the skin as you add it to the pan.

Ingredients for 2

3 to 4 cloves garlic
1 tbsp extra virgin olive oil
1 small onion, chopped
350g/12oz potatoes, peeled
   and diced
450ml/³/₄pt vegetable or
   chicken stock
salt and freshly ground
   black pepper
a little grated nutmeg
4 tbsp chopped fresh parsley
50g/2oz diced pancetta
   (optional)

Ingredients for 4

4 to 8 cloves garlic
2 tbsp extra virgin olive oil
1 large onion, chopped
700g/1¹/₂lb potatoes, peeled
   and diced
900ml/1¹/₂pt vegetable or
   chicken stock
salt and freshly ground
   black pepper
a little grated nutmeg
4 tbsp chopped fresh parsley
75g/3oz diced pancetta
   (optional)

1 Preheat the oven to 200°C/400°F/gas mark 6. Place the garlic cloves on a baking tray and roast for 10–20 minutes until soft.

2 Heat the olive oil in a saucepan and fry the onion and potatoes for 10 minutes until softened but not coloured.

3 Allow the garlic to cool slightly and then squeeze it from the skins into the pan.

4 Add the stock and bring to the boil. Reduce the heat and simmer for 20 minutes.

5 Purée the soup in a liquidizer or food processor and return to the pan. Season with salt, pepper and nutmeg.

6 Stir in the parsley and serve.

7 If desired, serve with a garnish of pancetta cubes, fried until crisp.

Sweet Potato Soup

vegetarian

A thick, warming soup that is perfect for winter evenings. Serve with chunks of Italian bread.

Ingredients for 2

15g/¹/₂oz butter
1 tbsp olive oil
1 small onion, chopped
1 clove garlic, chopped
250g/9oz sweet potato,
    peeled and cut into cubes
75g/3oz potatoes, peeled and
    cut into cubes
300ml/¹/₂pt vegetable stock
2 sprigs fresh thyme
150ml/¹/₄pt milk
salt and freshly ground
    black pepper
fresh thyme to garnish

Ingredients for 4

25g/1oz butter
2 tbsp olive oil
1 large onion, chopped
1 clove garlic, chopped
500g/1lb 2oz sweet potato,
    peeled and cut into cubes
175g/6oz potatoes, peeled
    and cut into cubes
600ml/1pt vegetable stock
2 to 3 sprigs fresh thyme
300ml/¹/₂pt milk
salt and freshly ground
    black pepper
fresh thyme to garnish

1 Heat the butter and oil in a large saucepan.

2 Fry the onion and garlic over a low heat for 5–10 minutes until softened.

3 Add the potatoes, stock and thyme.

4 Cover and simmer for 30 minutes.

5 Remove the thyme sprigs.

6 Purée the soup in a liquidizer or food processor and return to the pan.

7 Add the milk and heat gently. Season to taste with salt and pepper.

8 Serve garnished with a sprinkle of fresh thyme leaves.

Smoked Haddock Chowder with Sautéed Potato Croutes

This is a really filling soup, which is perfect on winter days. The addition of a generous helping of potato croutes makes this dish an economical, complete meal in one.

Ingredients for 2

1 tbsp butter
1/2 sweet pointed red pepper, seeded and chopped
1 tbsp plain flour
225ml/8fl oz vegetable or fish stock
225ml/8fl oz milk
100g/4oz waxy potatoes, peeled and diced
175g/6oz smoked haddock, skinned
200g/7oz can of creamed sweetcorn
salt and white pepper
pinch ground nutmeg

For the croutes:
175g/6oz waxy potatoes, peeled and diced
4 tbsp sunflower oil
1 tsp paprika

Ingredients for 4

25g/1oz butter
1 sweet pointed red pepper, seeded and chopped
25g/1oz plain flour
450ml/3/4pt vegetable or fish stock
450ml/3/4pt milk
225g/8oz waxy potatoes, peeled and diced
350g/12oz smoked haddock, skinned
418g/14 1/2 oz can of creamed sweetcorn
salt and white pepper
pinch ground nutmeg

For the croutes:
350g/12oz waxy potatoes, peeled and diced
4 tbsp sunflower oil
2 tsp paprika

1 Melt the butter in a pan and sauté the pepper for about 5 minutes until soft.

2 Stir in the flour and cook for a few seconds. Remove from the heat and gradually add the stock and milk. Return to the heat and cook, stirring constantly, until thickened slightly.

3 Add the potatoes and haddock. Simmer gently for 5 minutes. Break the fish up into flakes in the soup as it cooks. You can do this with the side of a fork or spoon.

4 Stir in the creamed sweetcorn and simmer for a further 5 minutes. Season to taste with salt, pepper and nutmeg.

5 Meanwhile, blanch the potatoes for the croutes in boiling water for 3–4 minutes, until just tender. Drain well.

6 Heat the oil in a frying pan and add the potatoes. Toss over a high heat until just golden. Stir in the paprika and toss over the heat for a few more seconds. Serve the soup with the potato croutes piled in the middle.

Rösti Tartlets with Tomatoes & Goat's Cheese

Easy Entertaining

The crisp, potato-based tartlet cases make an unusual alternative to this fashionable starter.

Ingredients for 2

225g/8oz waxy potatoes, peeled
1 tbsp flour
2 tbsp beaten egg
100g/4oz vine-ripened tomatoes, sliced
a few black olives
2 slices peppered goat's cheese
2 tsp extra virgin olive oil
1 tsp balsamic vinegar
salt and freshly ground black pepper

Ingredients for 4

450g/1lb waxy potatoes, peeled
2 tbsp flour
1 egg, lightly beaten
200g/7oz vine-ripened tomatoes, sliced
a few black olives
4 slices peppered goat's cheese
1 tbsp extra virgin olive oil
2 tsp balsamic vinegar
salt and freshly ground black pepper

1 Preheat the oven to 200°C/400°F/gas mark 6.

2 Coarsely grate the potatoes and place in a sieve. Put a small plate on the potatoes and press down, squeezing out as much moisture as you can.

3 Place the potatoes in a bowl and season with salt and pepper.

4 Sprinkle over the flour and add the egg. Mix well.

5 Divide the potatoes equally between two (four) shallow Yorkshire pudding tins, press the potato out with the back of a spoon to form a small tartlet case.

6 Bake for 20 minutes.

7 Arrange the tomato slices and olives in each tartlet case and return to the oven for 10 minutes, until the potatoes are crisp and the tomatoes softened.

8 Top with the goat's cheese. Drizzle with the olive oil and balsamic vinegar and serve.

Skinny Fries with Basil & Sun-blushed Tomato Dip

This is an indulgent snack that I like to serve as an occasional treat while watching a great film on the telly. Any leftover dip can be stored in the refrigerator for up to 2 days. The dip is fabulous in a ham and salad sarnie.

Fries for 2

**2 large floury potatoes,
    peeled
sunflower or ground nut oil
    for deep-frying
sea salt**

Fries for 4

**4 large floury potatoes,
    peeled
sunflower or ground nut oil
    for deep-frying
sea salt**

Basil & Sun-blushed Tomato Dip:

**25g/1oz fresh basil leaves
25g/1oz sun-blushed tomatoes, chopped
6 tbsp mayonnaise
4 tbsp natural yoghurt**

1 Make the dip by placing all the ingredients in a food processor and whizzing until blended.

2 Transfer to a serving bowl and chill until required.

3 Cut the potatoes into 6mm/¼in thick strips. Rinse in a colander to remove excess starch and pat dry on a clean tea towel.

4 Heat the oil to 190°C/375°F and cook the chips in two or three batches for about 5 minutes until golden brown.

5 Drain on kitchen paper and sprinkle with a little salt. Serve with the basil & sun-blushed tomato dip.

Crispy Potato Balls with Chilli Dip

I serve these spicy potato balls with a ready-made sweet chilli dipping sauce, but you could also serve them with a cucumber and yoghurt dip or mango chutney.

Ingredients for 2

150g/5oz floury potatoes, peeled
75g/3oz carrots, peeled
salt
50g/2oz frozen peas, thawed
1/2 red chilli, seeded and finely chopped
2 tbsp chopped fresh coriander
2 tbsp gram (chick-pea) flour
a little beaten egg
oil for deep-frying
sweet chilli sauce to serve

Ingredients for 4

300g/10½oz floury potatoes, peeled
150g/5oz carrots, peeled
salt
100g/4oz frozen peas, thawed
1 red chilli, seeded and finely chopped
4 tbsp chopped fresh coriander
4 tbsp gram (chick-pea) flour
a little beaten egg
oil for deep-frying
sweet chilli sauce to serve

1 Cut the potatoes and carrots into 2cm/³/₄in pieces. Bring a pan of water to the boil. Add a little salt and the potatoes and carrots and cook for 10 minutes until soft. Drain well.

2 Place in a bowl with the peas, chilli and coriander and mash well. Add the gram flour and enough egg to bind.

3 With damp hands shape the potato into small balls. Set aside.

4 Heat the oil for deep-frying to 180°C/350°F. Deep-fry the balls in batches until crisp and golden. Drain on kitchen paper and keep warm until all the balls are cooked.

5 Serve the potato balls with the chilli sauce for dipping.

Mixed Potato Crisps

Family Favourites

The hand-fried crisps available in the shops taste great but are expensive. Why not make your own? If you have a deep-fat fryer its very easy. I like to use a mixture of regular and sweet potatoes; occasionally I also fry slices of parsnip, beetroot and carrot.

Ingredients for 2

200g/7oz potatoes
100g/4oz sweet potatoes
oil for deep-frying
1/4 tsp dried thyme
sea salt, preferably Maldon
freshly ground black pepper

Ingredients for 4

400g/14oz potatoes
200g/7oz sweet potatoes
oil for deep-frying
1/2 tsp dried thyme
sea salt, preferably Maldon
freshly ground black pepper

1 Peel the potatoes and cut into very thin slices with a sharp knife, a mandolin or in a food processor.

2 Heat the oil for deep-fat frying to 190°C/375°F.

3 Deep-fry the potato slices in batches for 2–3 minutes until crisp and golden.

4 Remove the basket from the oil and shake off any excess oil. Tip the crisps onto a tray lined with kitchen paper.

5 Serve sprinkled with dried thyme, salt and pepper.

Potato Skins with Roasted Tomato Salsa

Both the salsa and the potato skins can be made in advance up to the end of step 5. They will then keep for up to 24 hours in the refrigerator. Use the potato flesh for any recipe requiring mash. Smoked paprika has a distinctive aroma and flavour, which works well in this salsa, but regular paprika can also be used.

Ingredients for 2

3 medium potatoes, scrubbed
75g/3oz plum tomatoes
25g/1oz spring onions, sliced
extra virgin olive oil
1 tsp lime juice
1/4 tsp smoked paprika

Ingredients for 4

5 large potatoes, scrubbed
150g/5oz plum tomatoes
50g/2oz spring onions, sliced
extra virgin olive oil
2 tsp lime juice
1/2 tsp smoked paprika

1 Preheat the oven to 190°C/375°F/gas mark 5. Prick the potato all over with a fork and bake for 1–1 1/4 hours until tender.

2 Meanwhile, cut the tomatoes in half and scoop out the seeds and discard. Dice the flesh. Place on a small baking sheet with the spring onions.

3 Drizzle with a little of the olive oil and roast below the potatoes for 15 minutes.

4 Transfer to a bowl and stir in the lime juice and paprika. Chill until required.

5 When the potatoes are cooked, leave to cool for a few minutes and then cut each into quarters lengthways. Scoop out the flesh with a spoon leaving just a small layer on the skin.

6 Brush the insides and outsides of the potato skins with olive oil and return to the oven for 20 minutes, or until crisp. Serve with the tomato salsa.

Sweet Potato Rösti with Peppered Beef

Easy Entertaining

Here the rosti is served with tender pieces of beef and soured cream to make an elegant starter. You could also serve the rosti as an accompaniment to a main course.

Ingredients for 2

225g/8oz sweet potatoes
1 egg, lightly beaten
1 tbsp plain flour
oil for shallow frying
**1/2 tsp coarsely ground
      black pepper**
175g/6oz rump steak
75ml/2¹/₂fl oz soured cream
1 tsp horseradish sauce
paprika to garnish

Ingredients for 4

450g/1lb sweet potatoes
2 eggs, lightly beaten
2 tbsp plain flour
oil for shallow frying
**1 tsp coarsely ground
      black pepper**
350g/12oz rump steak
150ml/¹/₄pt soured cream
2 tsp horseradish sauce
paprika to garnish

1 Peel and coarsely grate the sweet potato. Place in a mixing bowl with the eggs and flour. Mix until well combined.

2 Heat a little oil in a heavy-based frying pan. Add a few spoons of the potato mixture, spreading it out to form a small circle.

3 Cook for about 2 minutes each side until the rosti is crisp and golden. Place on absorbent kitchen paper and keep warm in the oven.

4 Repeat with the remaining mixture. You should be able to cook 2 or 3 at a time, depending on the size of your pan.

5 Press the pepper into the steak and grill under a hot grill for 3–4 minutes each side. Allow to stand for 5 minutes.

6 Stir the horseradish sauce into the soured cream.

7 Slice the beef thinly. Arrange the rosti on serving plates and top with some of the beef. Spoon on a little soured cream mix and sprinkle with a little paprika.

Potato Blinis with Smoked Trout

Easy Entertaining

The blinis can be kept warm on a plate over a pan of gently simmering water. They are ideal as a starter or as part of a hot buffet. If you use mashed potato that has had butter or milk added, you will need to add less liquid to the mixture. Smoked mackerel or smoked trout are also delicious with these little pancakes.

Ingredients for 2

150g/5oz mashed potatoes
1 egg
25g/1oz plain flour
about 2 tbsp milk
15g/^{1}/$_2$oz butter, melted
salt and freshly ground
**   black pepper**
a little olive oil
50g/2oz hot smoked trout
crème fraîche, to serve
chives, to garnish

Ingredients for 4

250g/9oz mashed potatoes
2 eggs
50g/2oz plain flour
about 4 tbsp milk
25g/1oz butter, melted
salt and freshly ground
**   black pepper**
a little olive oil
100g/4oz hot smoked salmon
crème fraîche, to serve
chives, to garnish

1 Place the potato in a mixing bowl. Beat the egg, flour, milk and melted butter into the potato until well combined. Season with salt and pepper.

2 Heat a little oil in a heavy-based frying pan to grease the pan. Spoon heaped tablespoons of the mixture into the pan and spread to form a small circle.

3 Cook for about 2 minutes until the underside is golden. Flip over and cook the other side.

4 Repeat with the remaining mixture until all the pancakes are made.

5 Serve the pancakes topped with a little smoked trout and a dollop of crème fraîche. Garnish with chives.

Mini Baked Potatoes with Rouille

Baked potatoes may be an all-time favourite, but here they are given a modern twist. You will find baby baking potatoes in the supermarket. Alternatively, choose small floury potatoes. The rouille will keep for up to 3 days in the refrigerator.

Ingredients for 2

12 baby baking potatoes
1 red pepper
1 red chilli, seeded if desired
1 clove garlic
1 tbsp fresh white
  breadcrumbs
1 tbsp extra virgin olive oil

Ingredients for 4

24 baby baking potatoes
2 red peppers
1 red chilli, seeded if desired
2 cloves garlic
2 tbsp fresh white
  breadcrumbs
2 tbsp extra virgin olive oil

1 Preheat the oven to 190°C/375°F/gas mark 5.

2 Scrub the potatoes, if required. Prick once or twice with a fork and place on a baking sheet. Bake for 40–45 minutes.

3 Meanwhile, place the peppers on a baking sheet and bake for 25 minutes at the top of the oven until the skins begin to blacken.

4 Place in a bowl, cover and leave for 5 minutes. Peel

the skin and discard, together with the core and seeds, but try to keep as much of the juice as possible.

5 Place the peppers, any juice, red chilli and garlic in a food processor and process until smooth. Add the breadcrumbs and oil and process again.

6 Serve the potatoes on cocktail sticks for dipping into the rouille. Alternatively, cut a small slice off each potato and spoon the rouille on top.

Feta and Mint Potato Crostini

You will get about 2 to 3 slices from each potato. Trimmings can be kept covered in salt water for up to 24 hours and used to make mash. The feta mixture can be made up to 12 hours ahead.

Ingredients for 2

50g/2oz feta cheese
extra virgin olive oil
1 tsp lemon juice
1 spring onion, chopped
2 tbsp chopped fresh mint
freshly ground black pepper
8 x 1cm/¹/₂in thick slices,
    taken from medium-size
    potatoes

Ingredients for 4

100g/4oz feta cheese
extra virgin olive oil
1 tbsp lemon juice
2 spring onions, chopped
4 tbsp chopped fresh mint
freshly ground black pepper
16 x 1cm/¹/₂in thick slices,
    taken from medium-size
    potatoes

1 Place the feta cheese in a small bowl and mash with a fork. Gradually beat in 1 (2) tbsp olive oil, the lemon juice, spring onions and mint. Season with pepper.

2 Blanch the potato slices in boiling water for 5 minutes. Drain well.

3 Heat a ridged griddle pan or heavy-based frying pan. Brush the potato slices on both sides with olive oil.

4 Cook for 3–4 minutes each side, until crisp and golden.

5 Pile the mint and feta mixture on top of the potato slices and serve immediately.

salads and light meals

New Potato Salad with Red Onion Dressing

This is a simple but very tasty basic salad in a light mayonnaise-style dressing.

Ingredients for 2

350g/12oz new potatoes
2 tbsp good mayonnaise
2 tbsp natural yoghurt
1/2 red onion, finely chopped
1 tbsp snipped fresh chives
salt and freshly ground
black pepper

Ingredients for 4

700g/1¹/₂lb new potatoes
4 tbsp good mayonnaise
4 tbsp natural yoghurt
1 red onion, finely chopped
2 tbsp snipped fresh chives
salt and freshly ground
black pepper

1 Peel or scrub the potatoes. Place in a saucepan with just enough water to cover.

2 Bring to the boil over a high heat, then reduce the heat and cook for 12–15 minutes until just tender. Drain.

3 Cool slightly. Peel if desired, then cut into bite-size pieces.

4 Combine the mayonnaise and yoghurt in a small bowl. Stir in the onion and chives. Season with salt and pepper.

5 Pour over the potatoes and toss gently to combine.

6 Serve at room temperature or lightly chilled.

Cypriote Potatoes

vegetarian

This is a delightful summer dish, perfect for alfresco eating.

Ingredients for 2

400g/14oz baby new
   potatoes, scrubbed
1 small red onion, cut
   into wedges
1 red pepper, sliced
2 tsp lemon juice
2 tsp tomato purée
4 tbsp olive oil
1 clove garlic, chopped
1/2 tsp dried oregano
100g/4oz vine-ripened
   tomatoes, quartered
100g/4oz haloumi cheese,
   crumbled into bite-size
   pieces
a small handful fresh mint
   leaves, roughly chopped

Ingredients for 4

700g/1½lb baby new
   potatoes, scrubbed
2 small red onions, cut
   into wedges
2 red peppers, sliced
1 tbsp lemon juice
1 tbsp tomato purée
100ml/3½fl oz olive oil
2 cloves garlic, chopped
1 tsp dried oregano
200g/7oz vine-ripened
   tomatoes, quartered
250g/9oz haloumi cheese,
   crumbled into bite-size
   pieces
a handful fresh mint leaves,
   roughly chopped

1 Preheat the oven to 200°C/400°F/gas mark 6.

2 Place the potatoes in a large bowl, with the onion and peppers.

3 Beat together the lemon juice, tomato purée, olive oil, garlic and oregano.

4 Pour over the potatoes and toss to coat. Spread the potatoes out on a large baking sheet and roast for 30 minutes, turning once.

5 Add the tomatoes and haloumi cheese. Toss together and roast for a further 10–15 minutes, or until the potatoes are just tender.

6 Remove from the oven. Sprinkle with mint leaves and serve.

Potato Salad Verdi

Tossed in a fabulous rocket-flavoured dressing, this potato salad is lighter and fresher than many traditional potato salads.

Ingredients for 2

350g/12oz baby new potatoes, scrubbed
25g/1oz rocket
25g/1oz watercress
2 shallots, roughly chopped
1 clove garlic, crushed
75ml/2½fl oz crème fraîche or full fat yoghurt
salt and freshly ground black pepper
freshly grated nutmeg

Ingredients for 4

700g/1½lb baby new potatoes, scrubbed
50g/2oz rocket
50g/2oz watercress
4 shallots, roughly chopped
2 cloves garlic, crushed
150ml/¼pt crème fraîche or full fat yoghurt
salt and freshly ground black pepper
freshly grated nutmeg

1 Bring a pan of water to the boil and cook the potatoes for 12–15 minutes, or until tender when pierced with a skewer.

2 Meanwhile, place the rocket, watercress, shallots, garlic, crème fraîche, or yoghurt, in a food processor and process until smooth.

3 Season with salt and pepper and a pinch of grated nutmeg.

4 Drain the potatoes well and allow to cool.

5 Toss the potatoes in the sauce and chill until required.

Piquant Potato Salad

A piquant dressing makes a change from the more usual mayonnaise dressing.

Ingredients for 2

**350g/12oz small new
    potatoes
3 tbsp olive oil
1 tbsp balsamic vinegar
1 clove garlic, crushed
3 spring onions, sliced
2 tbsp roughly chopped
    fresh flat-leaved parsley
25g/1oz black olives
25g/1oz caperberries
salt and freshly ground
    black pepper**

Ingredients for 4

**700g/1½lb small new
    potatoes
5 tbsp olive oil
2 tbsp balsamic vinegar
2 cloves garlic, crushed
6 spring onions, sliced
4 tbsp roughly chopped
    fresh flat-leaved parsley
50g/2oz black olives
50g/2oz caperberries
salt and freshly ground
    black pepper**

1 Preheat the oven to
200°C/400°F/gas 6.

2 Place the potatoes in a
roasting tin and drizzle
with 1 tbsp (2 tbsp) of the oil.
Sprinkle with a little salt. Roast
for 30 minutes, turning
occasionally until tender.

3 Whisk together the
remaining oil and the
vinegar, then stir in the garlic,
onion and parsley. Season with
salt and pepper.

4 Pour over the potatoes
and toss gently to
combine. Arrange the olives
and capers on top. Serve at
room temperature.

Italian Cracked Potato Salad

Potatoes cooked in their skins retain more nutrients. If you gently crack each potato open, the dressing will be absorbed into the potato flesh.

Ingredients for 2

**350g/12oz baby new
     potatoes**
150g/5oz mozzarella cheese
2 tbsp extra virgin olive oil
**½ small red onion, roughly
     chopped**
**1 or 2 sun-dried tomatoes,
     roughly chopped**
**a small handful fresh
     basil leaves**
1 tbsp red wine vinegar
4 black olives
**salt and freshly ground
     black pepper**

Ingredients for 4

**700g/1½lb baby new
     potatoes**
**300g/10½oz mozzarella
     cheese**
4 tbsp extra virgin olive oil
**1 small red onion, roughly
     chopped**
**3 sun-dried tomatoes,
     roughly chopped**
a handful fresh basil leaves
2 tbsp red wine vinegar
8 black olives
**salt and freshly ground
     black pepper**

1 Peel or scrub the potatoes. Place in a saucepan with just enough water to cover.

2 Bring to the boil over a high heat. Reduce the heat and cook for 12–15 minutes, or until just tender. Drain and allow to cool.

3 Meanwhile, tear the mozzarella into bite-size pieces.

4 Place the oil, onion, sun-dried tomatoes, basil and vinegar in a food processor and chop finely.

5 Lightly crack open each potato with a fork and toss them in the onion and basil mixture.

6 Arrange on a dish and add the cheese and olives. Season with salt and pepper.

Brie, Artichoke and Potato Salad

This makes a fabulous light summer meal, perfect for alfresco eating.

Ingredients for 2

250g/9oz small new potatoes, scrubbed
75g/3oz cherry tomatoes
200g/7oz can artichoke hearts, rinsed and drained
4 spring onions, trimmed and thinly sliced
2 tbsp extra virgin olive oil
1 tbsp lemon juice
25g/1oz rocket
100g/4oz Brie, sliced
salt and freshly ground black pepper

Ingredients for 4

500g/1lb 2oz small new potatoes, scrubbed
150g/5oz cherry tomatoes
400g/14oz can artichoke hearts, rinsed and drained
8 spring onions, trimmed and thinly sliced
4 tbsp extra virgin olive oil
2 tbsp lemon juice
50g/2oz rocket
200g/7oz Brie, sliced
salt and freshly ground black pepper

1 Place the potatoes in a saucepan and add enough water to just cover. Cover the pan, place over a high heat and bring to the boil.

2 Salt the water, reduce the heat and simmer for 15–20 minutes until just tender. Drain well.

3 Transfer the potatoes to a large bowl and cut into bite-size pieces, if required. Allow to cool.

4 Halve the cherry tomatoes.

5 Quarter the artichoke hearts and add to the bowl with the onion and tomatoes.

6 Mix together the oil and lemon juice and season with salt and pepper. Pour over the potatoes and toss until well coated.

7 Just before serving, arrange the rocket leaves and Brie on individual serving plates. Add the potato salad and serve.

Smoked Mackerel and Dill Salad

Serve as a light main meal salad or serve smaller portions as a starter to a meal.

Ingredients for 2

450g/1lb new potatoes
100g/4oz cucumber
200g/7oz smoked peppered mackerel
2 tbsp olive oil
2 tbsp white wine vinegar
1 tbsp chopped fresh dill
sea salt

Ingredients for 4

900g/2lb new potatoes
200g/7oz cucumber
400g/14oz smoked peppered mackerel
4 tbsp olive oil
4 tbsp white wine vinegar
2 tbsp chopped fresh dill
sea salt

1 Place the potatoes in a saucepan and add enough water to just cover. Cover the pan, place over a high heat and bring to the boil.

2 Salt the water, reduce the heat and simmer for 15–20 minutes until just tender. Drain well. Halve or quarter, depending on the size.

3 Cut the cucumber in half lengthwise and scoop out the seeds. Peel, if desired. Cut in half again lengthwise, then cut into 1cm/1/2in thick slices. Add to the potatoes.

4 Flake the fish into large chunks. Add to the potatoes.

5 Whisk together the oil, vinegar and dill. Pour over the potatoes and toss to coat. Take care not to break up the fish too much. Serve immediately.

Warm Potato Salad with Bacon and Broad Beans

A perfect salad for cooler days.

Ingredients for 2

350g/12oz new potatoes
3 rashers back bacon
100g/4oz frozen broad beans
2 tbsp olive oil
1 small onion, sliced
1 tsp brown sugar
1 tsp wholegrain mustard
2 tbsp white wine vinegar
1 hard-boiled egg, quartered
salt and freshly ground
**   black pepper**

Ingredients for 4

700g/1½lb new potatoes
6 rashers back bacon
225g/8oz frozen broad beans
4 tbsp olive oil
1 large onion, sliced
2 tsp brown sugar
2 tsp wholegrain mustard
4 tbsp white wine vinegar
2 hard-boiled eggs,
**   quartered**
salt and freshly ground
**   black pepper**

1 Place the potatoes in a saucepan and add enough water to just cover. Cover the pan, place over a high heat and bring to the boil.

2 Salt the water, reduce the heat and simmer for 15–20 minutes until just tender. Drain well. Peel and cut the potatoes into large dice.

3 Remove the rind from the bacon and cut the bacon into thick strips. Cook the beans in boiling water for 5 minutes. Drain.

4 Meanwhile, heat the oil in a large frying pan, or wok, and fry the onion and bacon for 5 minutes until the onion is beginning to colour.

5 Add the cooked potatoes and toss over the heat for a minute or two. Sprinkle over the sugar, add the beans and toss until well combined.

6 Add the mustard and vinegar. Season with salt and pepper. Remove from the heat, toss again and serve immediately with the hard-boiled eggs arranged on top.

Creamy Potato Salad

Family Favourite

The thick, creamy potato salads that I remember from my childhood were very thick and heavy, or else made with salad cream. Here I have updated this much-loved salad with a much lighter sauce.

Ingredients for 2

400g/14oz potatoes, peeled
1/2 small red pepper, seeded
4 spring onions
50g/2oz frozen peas, thawed
50g/2oz sweetcorn kernels,
    thawed if frozen
75ml/2¹/2fl oz mayonnaise
4 tbsp reduced-fat crème
    fraîche
1/2 tsp paprika
salt and freshly ground
    black pepper

Ingredients for 4

800g/1lb 12oz potatoes,
    peeled
1 small red pepper, seeded
8 spring onions
100g/4oz frozen peas, thawed
100g/4oz sweetcorn kernels,
    thawed if frozen
150ml/5fl oz mayonnaise
100ml/3¹/2fl oz reduced-fat
    crème fraîche
1 tsp paprika
salt and freshly ground
    black pepper

1 Cook the potatoes in lightly salted boiling water for 15 minutes, or until just tender.

2 Drain and then rinse under running cold water to cool. Cut into dice.

3 Cut the pepper into dice.

4 Thickly slice the spring onions.

5 Place all the ingredients in a large bowl and toss to combine. Chill until required.

Potato and Prawn Salad

A reworking of the classic prawn cocktail, this salad is more filling and makes a great light meal.

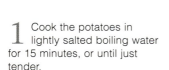

Ingredients for 2

350g/12oz new potatoes
3 tbsp mayonnaise
3 tbsp natural yoghurt
1/4 tsp grated lime zest
1 tsp lime juice
1/4 tsp grated root ginger
25g/1oz mange tout
100g/4oz tiger prawns
rocket leaves, to serve

Ingredients for 4

700g/1 1/2lb new potatoes
75ml/2 1/2fl oz mayonnaise
75ml/2 1/2fl oz natural yoghurt
1/2 tsp grated lime zest
2 tsp lime juice
1/2 tsp grated root ginger
25g/1oz mange tout
225g/8oz prawns
rocket leaves, to serve

1 Cook the potatoes in lightly salted boiling water for 15 minutes, or until just tender.

2 Drain and rinse under running cold water to cool. Cut into bite-size pieces.

3 Mix together the mayonnaise, yoghurt, lime zest, juice and ginger.

4 Blanch the mange tout in boiling water for 1 minute and then cool quickly under cold water. Drain.

5 Stir the mange tout, potatoes and prawns into the lime mayonnaise.

6 Chill for at least 30 minutes.

7 Pile the rocket leaves onto individual plates and spoon the salad to the side.

Cheesy Potato Fritters

vegetarian

These tasty potato bites are well worth the effort. They make a great light meal served with a little salad. You can also serve them as an accompaniment to steak or chicken.

Ingredients for 2

250g/9oz potatoes, peeled
50g/2oz plain flour
1/2 tsp bicarbonate of soda
1/4 tsp vinegar
75ml/2¹/₂fl oz water
50g/2oz grated cheese
    (Cheddar, Emmenthal or
    Gouda)
1 tbsp seasoned flour
oil for deep-frying

Ingredients for 4

500g/1lb 2oz potatoes,
    peeled
100g/4oz plain flour
1 tsp bicarbonate of soda
1/2 tsp vinegar
150ml/¹/₄pt water
100g/4oz grated cheese
    (Cheddar, Emmenthal or
    Gouda)
2 tbsp seasoned flour
oil for deep-frying

1 Slice the potatoes about 3mm/1/2in thick. Rinse to remove excess starch, drain and pat dry with kitchen paper.

2 Sift the flour and bicarbonate of soda into a bowl. Add the vinegar and then slowly whisk in the water to form a smooth batter.

3 Sandwich together two potato slices with a little cheese in the middle. Repeat until you have used up all the cheese. Dust with seasoned flour. Dust any remaining potato slices with seasoned flour.

4 Heat the oil to 170°C/325°F, or until a piece of bread turns golden in 1 minute.

5 Dip the potato sandwiches and plain potato slices into the batter and drop into the hot fat, a few at a time. Cooking in batches, fry for 45 minutes until crisp and golden.

6 Drain on kitchen paper and serve immediately.

Turkey Croquettes

This is one of my favourite ways of using leftover turkey after Christmas. However, you can also use leftover chicken from the Sunday roast.

Ingredients for 2

175g/6oz leftover cooked turkey
200g/7oz potatoes, cooked and mashed
1 tsp olive oil
1/2 small onion, finely chopped
2 rashers streaky bacon, chopped
1/2 tsp dried sage
salt and pepper
flour to dust
1 egg, lightly beaten
25g/1oz dried breadcrumbs
oil for shallow frying

Ingredients for 4

350g/12oz leftover cooked turkey
400g/14oz potatoes, cooked and mashed
2 tsp olive oil
1 small onion, finely chopped
4oz/100g streaky bacon, chopped
1 tsp dried sage
salt and pepper
flour to dust
1 egg, lightly beaten
50g/2oz dried breadcrumbs
oil for shallow frying

1 Finely chop the cooked turkey. Place in a mixing bowl with the mashed potato.

2 Heat the olive oil in a frying pan and sauté the onion and bacon until the onion is softened.

3 Add to the bowl. Add the sage and season with salt and pepper. Beat until well blended. Shape into 4 (8) logs. Dust with flour.

4 Dip into the beaten egg and coat with breadcrumbs.

5 Wipe out the frying pan with kitchen paper and heat enough oil for shallow frying. Gently fry the croquettes for 8–10 minutes, or until crisp and golden on the outside.

Salmon Fish Cakes

Family Favourite

Fish cakes are one of the few ways that I can get my children to eat fish, especially oily fish, which contains the important Omega 3 oils. When they taste this good, you can understand why.

Ingredients for 2

350g/12oz potatoes, peeled and cut into small chunks
200g/7oz salmon fillet, skinned
1 tbsp snipped chives
sunflower oil for frying
salt and freshly ground black pepper

Ingredients for 4

700g/1½lb potatoes, peeled and cut into small chunks
400g/14oz salmon fillet, skinned
2 tbsp snipped chives
sunflower oil for frying
salt and freshly ground black pepper

1 Cook the potatoes in lightly salted boiling water for 10–15 minutes until just tender.

2 Meanwhile, place the fish in a small pan and add enough water to cover. Poach for 5 minutes, or until the fish flakes easily. Alternatively, cook the fish in the microwave about 2–3 minutes for two people and 4–5 minutes for four people.

3 Drain the salmon, reserving 2 tbsp (4 tbsp) of the cooking liquor, and flake the flesh, discarding any bones.

4 Drain the potatoes well, mash and mix with the fish, reserved liquor and chives, until well combined. Season to taste.

5 Shape the mixture into 4 (8) rounds.

6 Heat the oil in a frying pan and shallow-fry for 5–10 minutes until heated through and crisp.

Baked Spanish Omelette

Quick and Easy

Even if you have never made an omelette before, this baked version is simplicity itself. It is hard to reduce the quantity for two, but it is fabulous served cold, so any left over can be kept in the fridge and eaten the next day.

Serves 4

2 tbsp grated Parmesan cheese
450g/1lb potatoes, peeled and sliced
2 tbsp sunflower oil
1 onion, peeled and sliced
2 tbsp chopped fresh flat-leaved parsley
6 eggs
4 tbsp milk
pinch grated nutmeg
salt and freshly ground black pepper

1 Preheat the oven to 180°C/350°F/gas mark 4.

2 Lightly grease and line the base of a 20cm/8in round cake tin. (If using a loose-bottom tin, line the base and side with foil to prevent the mixture from running out.) Sprinkle the surface of the tin with Parmesan cheese.

3 Place the potatoes in a pan of boiling water and simmer for 5 minutes until just tender. Drain well and set aside.

4 Heat the oil in a small frying pan and fry the onion for about 4 minutes until soft.

5 Remove from the heat and stir in the parsley.

6 Arrange half the potato in the prepared tin. Then spread the onion mixture over. Top with the remaining potato.

7 Beat the eggs and milk together and season lightly with salt, pepper and nutmeg.

8 Pour into the tin and bake for 25–30 minutes until golden and set. Serve hot or cold, cut into wedges.

Gnocchi with Fresh Tomato Sauce

Made from humble ingredients yet very filling; economical and tasty too.

Ingredients for 2

Gnocchi:
250g/9oz floury potatoes
50g/2oz plain flour
1 egg yolk
a few fresh basil leaves

Sauce:
1 tbsp extra virgin oil
1/2 small onion, chopped
**225g/8oz tomatoes, seeded
and chopped**
**salt and freshly ground
black pepper**

Ingredients for 4

Gnocchi:
500g/1lb 2oz floury potatoes
100g/4oz plain flour
2 egg yolks
a small handful basil leaves

Sauce:
2 tbsp extra virgin oil
1 small onion, chopped
**450g/1lb tomatoes, seeded
and chopped**
**salt and freshly ground
black pepper**

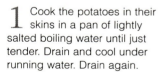

1 Cook the potatoes in their skins in a pan of lightly salted boiling water until just tender. Drain and cool under running water. Drain again.

2 Peel the potatoes and mash well. Add the flour and egg yolks. Chop the basil and add to the bowl. Season well. Beat until well combined to form a soft dough.

3 Working on a floured surface, take pieces of the dough and roll into a rope about 1cm/1/2in thick. Cut into pieces about 2cm/1in long.

Roll each piece over the tines of a fork to mark. Set aside while preparing the sauce.

4 Heat the oil in a saucepan and sauté the onion for 5 minutes until softened. Add the tomatoes and cook gently for 10 minutes. Season.

5 To cook the gnocchi bring a large saucepan of water to the boil. Add the gnocchi and simmer until they float to the top. Remove with a draining spoon and transfer to a warm serving dish. Spoon the tomato sauce on top.

Gnocchi with Fresh Tomato Sauce

Made from humble ingredients yet very filling; economical and tasty too.

Ingredients for 2

Gnocchi:
250g/9oz floury potatoes
50g/2oz plain flour
1 egg yolk
a few fresh basil leaves

Sauce:
1 tbsp extra virgin oil
$\frac{1}{2}$ small onion, chopped
225g/8oz tomatoes, seeded
**   and chopped**
salt and freshly ground
**   black pepper**

Ingredients for 4

Gnocchi:
500g/1lb 2oz floury potatoes
100g/4oz plain flour
2 egg yolks
a small handful basil leaves

Sauce:
2 tbsp extra virgin oil
1 small onion, chopped
450g/1lb tomatoes, seeded
**   and chopped**
salt and freshly ground
**   black pepper**

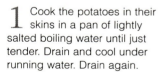

1 Cook the potatoes in their skins in a pan of lightly salted boiling water until just tender. Drain and cool under running water. Drain again.

2 Peel the potatoes and mash well. Add the flour and egg yolks. Chop the basil and add to the bowl. Season well. Beat until well combined to form a soft dough.

3 Working on a floured surface, take pieces of the dough and roll into a rope about 1cm/½in thick. Cut into pieces about 2cm/1in long.

Roll each piece over the tines of a fork to mark. Set aside while preparing the sauce.

4 Heat the oil in a saucepan and sauté the onion for 5 minutes until softened. Add the tomatoes and cook gently for 10 minutes. Season.

5 To cook the gnocchi bring a large saucepan of water to the boil. Add the gnocchi and simmer until they float to the top. Remove with a draining spoon and transfer to a warm serving dish. Spoon the tomato sauce on top.

Bubble and Squeak

Bacon Rösti with Creamy Mushrooms

The creamy mushrooms served with the rösti could also be tossed with plain boiled new potatoes. Choose a mixture of mushrooms, such as button, chestnut and oyster mushrooms.

Ingredients for 2

175g/6oz mixed mushrooms
1 tbsp olive oil
75g/3oz garlic and herb
    cream cheese
2 tbsp milk

Rösti:

1 tbsp olive oil, plus extra for
    oiling
1/2 small onion, chopped
4 rashers smoked streaky,
    rind removed and
    chopped
350g/12oz waxy potatoes,
    peeled
2 tbsp plain flour
1 small egg, lightly beaten
salt and freshly ground
    black pepper

Ingredients for 4

350g/12oz mixed mushrooms
2 tbsp olive oil
150g/5 oz garlic and herb
    cream cheese
4 tbsp milk

Rösti:

1 tbsp olive oil, plus extra for
    oiling
1 small onion, chopped
8 rashers smoked streaky,
    rind removed and
    chopped
700g/1^{1}/2lb oz waxy potatoes,
    peeled
3 tbsp plain flour
1 large egg, lightly beaten
salt and freshly ground
    black pepper

1 To prepare the rösti, heat the oil in a large frying pan and fry the onion and bacon for 5–8 minutes until the onion is softened and just beginning to colour. Allow to cool.

2 Coarsely grate the potato and place in a sieve. Put a saucer or small plate on top and press down, squeezing out as much liquid as you can.

3 Add the bacon mixture to the grated potatoes. Sprinkle over the flour and then add the egg. Season and mix well.

4 Slice the mushrooms. Heat the oil in a small pan and fry for 3–4 minutes until tender.

5 Add the cream cheese and milk and cook gently, stirring until the cheese melts and forms a sauce. Keep warm.

6 Heat a large heavy-based pan or flat griddle and lightly oil the surface. Divide the potato mixture into 2 (4). Spoon

one portion into the pan and spread to form a circle. Cook until the underside is dark golden and crisp.

7 Flip over and cook the other side. Allow about 3 minutes each side. Drain in kitchen paper and keep warm while cooking the remainder.

8 Serve the rösti topped with the creamy mushrooms

Jacket Potatoes with Mediterranean Roast Vegetables

Fluffy potato in a crispy shell topped with roasted vegetables makes a perfect combination.

Ingredients for 2

- 2 baking potatoes about 275g/10oz each
- 1/4 small aubergine, cut into chunks
- 1 small courgette, cut into thick slices
- 1/2 red onion, cut into wedges
- 1/2 red pepper, seeded and cut into chunks
- 1/2 yellow pepper, seeded and cut into chunks
- 1 plum tomato, quartered
- 1 clove garlic, sliced
- 1 tbsp olive oil
- 1 tsp chopped fresh rosemary
- 50g/2oz mozzarella cheese, cut into cubes
- salt and freshly ground black pepper

Ingredients for 4

- 4 baking potatoes about 275g/10oz each
- 1/2 small aubergine, cut into chunks
- 1 courgette, cut into thick slices
- 1 red onion, cut into wedges
- 1 red pepper, seeded and cut into chunks
- 1 yellow pepper, seeded and cut into chunks
- 2 plum tomatoes, quartered
- 1 clove garlic, sliced
- 2 tbsp olive oil
- 1 tbsp chopped fresh rosemary
- 100g/4oz mozzarella cheese, cut into cubes
- salt and freshly ground black pepper

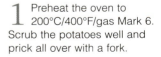

1

1 Preheat the oven to 200°C/400°F/gas Mark 6. Scrub the potatoes well and prick all over with a fork.

2 Place on a baking sheet and bake near the top of the oven for 1 1/2 hours, turning once.

3

3 Spread the prepared vegetables and garlic in a roasting tin. Sprinkle with olive oil and rosemary. Season with salt and pepper.

4 Roast the vegetables below the potatoes for 45–50 minutes until soft and beginning to char at the edges.

5 When cooked, cut a large cross into the potatoes and squeeze to open out.

6 Divide the cheese between the potatoes.

7 Place on a serving plate and serve topped with the roasted vegetables.

6

Sate Jackets

Family Favourite

Jacket potatoes are always a great standby.

Ingredients for 2

2 baking potatoes
1 chicken breast, skinned
** and boned**
1 tbsp sunflower oil
1/2 tsp caster sugar
1/4 tsp ground cumin
1/4 tsp ground coriander
large pinch chilli powder
1 tbsp soy sauce
4 tbsp peanut butter

Ingredients for 4

4 baking potatoes
2 chicken breasts, skinned
** and boned**
2 tbsp sunflower oil
1 tsp caster sugar
1/2 tsp ground cumin
1/2 tsp ground coriander
1/4 tsp chilli powder
2 tbsp soy sauce
8 tbsp peanut butter

1 Preheat the oven to 200°C/400°F/gas Mark 6. Scrub the potatoes well and prick all over with a fork.

2 Place on a baking sheet and bake near the top of the oven for 1 1/2 hours, turning once.

3 Meanwhile, cut the chicken lengthways into thin strips and thread, concertina style, onto small wooden skewers.

4 Mix together the oil, sugar, spices and soy sauce. Pour over the chicken and turn so that the strips are coated in the mixture. Chill until required.

5 About 15 minutes before the potatoes are cooked, place the chicken on a baking sheet and bake for 20 minutes, or until cooked through.

6 When the potatoes are tender, cut the tops off them and scoop out the flesh. Mash with the peanut butter and return to the potato shells. Return to the oven for 10 minutes and then serve with the chicken skewers.

main meal
magic

Beef Pot-roast

One Pot

A mixture of main crop and sweet potatoes stretch the meat so that a little goes a long way in this super one-pot meal. Even if you are cooking the smaller quantity, you may have some meat left over but do not worry, it is delicious served cold.

Ingredients for 2

400g/14oz rolled brisket
1 tbsp sunflower oil
100g/4oz shallots, peeled
225g/8oz sweet potato,
    peeled and cut into
    large chunks
175g/6oz main crop
    potatoes, peeled and cut
    into large chunks
200ml/7fl oz beef stock
2 cloves garlic, peeled
salt and freshly ground
    black pepper

Ingredients for 4

700g/1½lb rolled brisket
2 tbsp sunflower oil
225g/8oz shallots, peeled
450g/1lb sweet potato,
    peeled and cut into
    large chunks
350g/12oz main crop
    potatoes, peeled and
    cut into large chunks
300ml/½pt beef stock
6 cloves garlic, peeled
salt and freshly ground
    black pepper

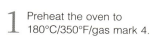

1 Preheat the oven to 180°C/350°F/gas mark 4.

2 Season the meat with salt and pepper.

3 Heat the oil in a flameproof casserole and brown the meat quickly on all sides.

4 Add all the remaining ingredients. Cover and cook in the oven for 1½–2 hours depending on the size of the meat.

5 Transfer the meat and vegetables to a serving plate and serve the gravy separately in a jug.

Shepherd's Pie

Family Favourite

A classic all-time family favourite.

Ingredients for 2

2 tsp sunflower oil
1 small onion, chopped
1 clove garlic, chopped
250g/9oz lean minced lamb
1/2 tsp dried mixed herbs
2 tsp plain flour
150ml/1/4pt lamb or vegetable
  stock
2 tsp Worcestershire sauce
450g/1lb floury potatoes,
  peeled and cut into
  chunks
splash milk
knob butter
40g/1 1/2oz Cheddar cheese
  (optional)
salt and freshly ground
  black pepper

Ingredients for 4

1 tbsp sunflower oil
1 large onion, chopped
1 clove garlic, chopped
500g/1lb 2oz lean minced lamb
1 tsp dried mixed herbs
1 tbsp plain flour
300ml/1/2pt lamb or vegetable
  stock
1 tbsp Worcestershire sauce
900g/2lb floury potatoes,
  peeled and cut into
  chunks
4 tbsp milk
25g/1oz butter
50g/2oz Cheddar cheese
  (optional)
salt and freshly ground
  black pepper

1 Heat the oil in a large saucepan and fry the onion and garlic until softened.

2 Add the mince and cook, breaking up the mince with the side of a spoon, until browned.

3 Stir in the herbs and flour.

4 Gradually add the stock and Worcestershire sauce, stirring until thickened slightly. Reduce heat and simmer while preparing the topping.

5 Heat the oven to 190°C/375°F/gas mark 5.

6 Cook the potatoes in lightly salted boiling water for 12–15 minutes until tender.

7 Drain and return to the pan. Add the milk and butter and season. Mash well.

8 Season the meat to taste and pour into an ovenproof baking dish. Spoon off any excess fat.

9 Carefully spread the mashed potato on top of the mince, fluffing it with a fork.

10 Sprinkle the cheese over the top, if using. Bake for 25 minutes, or until the potato is crisp and golden.

Potato Moussaka

Family Favourite

Moussaka is a classic Greek dish, which is usually made with layers of aubergine. Here, it has been adapted to use potatoes, which absorb less oil, making it a lower fat alternative to the traditional version.

Ingredients for 2

300g/10½oz potatoes, peeled and thinly sliced
2 tsp olive oil
1 small onion, finely chopped
1 clove garlic, chopped
250g/9oz lean minced beef
1 heaped tbsp tomato purée
2 tbsp red wine or water
25g/1oz butter
25g/1oz plain flour
300ml/½pt milk
1 egg
75g/3oz Cheddar cheese, grated
salt and ground pepper

Ingredients for 4

500g/1lb 2oz potatoes, peeled and thinly sliced
1 tbsp olive oil
1 onion, finely chopped
2 cloves garlic, chopped
500g/1lb 2oz lean minced beef
3 tbsp tomato purée
4 tbsp red wine or water
50g/2oz butter
50g/2oz plain flour
600ml/1pt milk
2 eggs
75g/3oz Cheddar cheese, grated
salt and ground pepper

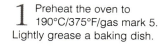

1 Preheat the oven to 190°C/375°F/gas mark 5. Lightly grease a baking dish.

2 Blanch the potatoes in boiling water for 3 minutes. Drain.

3 Heat the oil in a frying pan and fry onion and garlic until soft. Add mince and cook until browned, breaking it up as it cooks.

4 Stir in the tomato purée and red wine or water. Season with salt and pepper. Remove from the heat and set aside.

5 Melt the butter in a saucepan, stir in the flour, cook for 30 seconds and remove from the heat.

6 Gradually stir in the milk and return to the heat. Cook, stirring constantly, until the sauce thickens. Season well.

7 Lightly beat the eggs to break up. Beat them into the white sauce.

8 Layer potato and meat mixture alternately in the dish, finishing with a layer of potato.

9 Pour sauce over the top and sprinkle with grated cheese. Bake in the centre of the oven for 45 minutes.

Beer and Beef Hotpot

Family Favourite

A warming winter meal that is perfect for colder days. Just add a fresh green vegetable for a complete meal.

Ingredients for 2

1 tbsp sunflower oil, plus
   extra for brushing
1 onion, sliced
250g/9oz lean braising steak,
   cut into cubes
15g/¹⁄₂oz plain flour
150ml/¹⁄₄pt brown ale
175ml/6fl oz beef stock
¹⁄₄ tsp caster sugar
100g/4oz mushrooms, sliced
100g/4oz carrots, sliced
500g/1lb 2oz potatoes, peeled
salt and freshly ground
   black pepper

Ingredients for 4

2 tbsp sunflower oil, plus
   extra for brushing
1 large onion, sliced
500g/1lb 2oz lean braising
   steak, cut into cubes
25g/1oz plain flour
300ml/¹⁄₂pt brown ale
450ml/³⁄₄pt beef stock
¹⁄₂ tsp caster sugar
225g/8oz mushrooms, sliced
225g/8oz carrots, sliced
1kg/2¹⁄₄lb potatoes, peeled
salt and freshly ground
   black pepper

1 Heat the oil a in a large pan and gently fry the onion until it begins to soften. Add the meat and cook until browned on all sides.

2 Sprinkle the flour into the pan and cook for a few seconds. Stir in the ale and stock and bring to the boil, stirring. Add the sugar. Simmer for 30 minutes.

3 Preheat the oven to 170°C/325°F/gas mark 3.

4 Stir in the mushrooms and carrots. Season with salt and pepper. Thickly slice the potatoes. Place a layer of potatoes in the bottom of a deep ovenproof casserole. Spoon some of the meat mixture over the potatoes. Repeat layers, finishing with a layer of potatoes.

5 Brush the top of the potatoes with a little oil. Cover with foil and bake for 1 hour. Remove the foil and bake for a further 30 minutes, or until the meat is tender and the potatoes are golden.

Spring Lamb Casserole

One Pot

Cooked in the casserole the potatoes absorb the flavour of the meat, making this a delicious meal in one.

Ingredients for 2

1 tbsp sunflower oil
4 lean lamb chops
225g/8oz new carrots,
    scraped and cut in
    half if large
250g/8oz baby new potatoes
300ml/¹⁄₂pt vegetable or
    lamb stock
1 sprig fresh thyme
1 sprig rosemary
bay leaf
100g/4oz shelled broad beans
salt and freshly ground
    black pepper
chopped fresh parsley, to
    garnish (optional)

Ingredients for 4

2 tbsp sunflower oil
8 lean lamb chops
450g/1lb new carrots,
    scraped and cut in
    half if large
500g/1lb 2oz baby new
    potatoes
600ml/1pt vegetable or
    lamb stock
2 sprigs fresh thyme
2 sprigs rosemary
bay leaf
225g/8oz shelled broad beans
salt and freshly ground
    black pepper
chopped fresh parsley, to
    garnish (optional)

1 Heat the oil in a heavy-based pan and fry the meat until browned on both sides.

2 Add the carrots and potatoes and toss well. Stir in the stock and herbs. Season with salt and pepper.

3 Bring gently to the boil, cover and simmer gently for 45 minutes.

4 Add the broad beans. Continue to cook for 20 minutes until the lamb is done and all the vegetables are tender.

5 Remove herb sprigs and sprinkle with chopped parsley to serve, if desired.

Roast Lamb with Potatoes Boulangere

Easy Entertaining

This classic French dish gets its name from the days when the Sunday roast was taken to the local baker to be cooked in his ovens. You can place the lamb directly on the potatoes but I prefer to place it directly on the oven shelf above. The juices will still drop into the potatoes but in this way you get the maximum amount of crispy potatoes on the top, which I love.

Ingredients for 4 to 6

½ **leg lamb about 1 kg/2¼lb in weight**
1 clove garlic, sliced
1 onion, thinly sliced
700g/1½lb waxy potatoes
salt and white pepper
¼ tsp dried thyme
150ml/¼pt hot beef, chicken or vegetable stock
25g/1oz butter

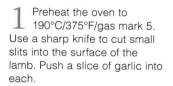

1 Preheat the oven to 190°C/375°F/gas mark 5. Use a sharp knife to cut small slits into the surface of the lamb. Push a slice of garlic into each.

2 Peel and thinly slice the potatoes, ideally with a mandolin or the slicing attachment of a food processor. Rinse and pat dry.

3 Lightly grease a shallow baking dish and place a layer of potatoes in it. Place a layer of onions on top. Repeat the layers, finishing with a layer of potato. Season each layer with salt, pepper and a little of the thyme.

4 Pour the stock over the potatoes and dot the top with butter. Place in the oven with the lamb directly on the shelf above, so that the juices of the lamb will drop onto the potatoes.

5 Roast the lamb for 1¼ hours and the potatoes for 1½ hours. Leave the lamb in a warm place while the potatoes finish cooking, about 15 minutes.

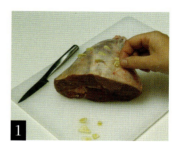

Lamb Hotpot

One Pot

This must be one of the simplest casserole dishes to put together. You can brown the meat first but I do not find it absolutely necessary.

Ingredients for 2

250g/9oz lean lamb, cubed
450g/1lb potatoes, sliced
100g/4oz carrots, sliced
100g/4oz parsnips, sliced
150ml/¹/₄pt lamb or beef
  stock
salt and freshly ground
  black pepper
a little oil for brushing

Ingredients for 4

500g/1lb 2oz lean lamb,
  cubed
900g/2lb potatoes, sliced
225g/8oz carrots, sliced
225g/8oz parsnips, sliced
300ml/¹/₂pt lamb or beef
  stock
salt and freshly ground
  black pepper
a little oil for brushing

1 Preheat the oven to 180°C/350°F/gas mark 4.

2 Layer the meat and vegetables in a deep ovenproof casserole dish, starting and finishing with potato. Lightly season the layers with salt and pepper.

3 Carefully pour the stock over so that it seeps into the layers.

4 Brush the top with a little oil.

5 Bake for 1¹/₂–2 hours, until the meat and vegetables are tender.

6 If the top begins to brown too much before the end of the cooking time, cover with foil.

Grilled Pork with Rösti Wedges and Apple Sauce

Serve with green beans for a simple meal.

Ingredients for 2

- 300g/10½oz waxy potatoes, peeled
- 1 small onion, very finely chopped
- 1 clove garlic, chopped
- 1 tbsp plain flour
- 1 egg, lightly beaten
- 15g/½oz butter
- 1 tbsp olive oil
- 2 pork chops
- apple sauce to serve
- salt and freshly ground black pepper

Ingredients for 4

- 600g/1lb 5oz waxy potatoes, peeled
- 1 onion, very finely chopped
- 1 clove garlic, chopped
- 2 tbsp plain flour
- 2 eggs, lightly beaten
- 25g/1oz butter
- 2 tbsp olive oil
- 4 pork chops
- apple sauce to serve
- salt and freshly ground black pepper

1 To make the rösti, coarsely grate the potato and place in a sieve. Put a saucer or small plate on top and press down, squeezing out as much liquid as you can.

2 Stir the onion and garlic into the potato. Sprinkle with flour. Add the eggs and season with salt and pepper. Mix well.

3 Heat the butter and oil in an 18cm/7in (20cm/8in) frying pan. Spread the potato mixture into the pan and flatten into one large round.

4 Cook over a low heat for 10 minutes. Place a plate over the pan and flip the rösti out onto the plate. Slide it back into the pan and cook for a further 10 minutes until both sides are crisp and golden.

5 Slide the rösti out of the pan and cut into wedges to serve.

6 Meanwhile, cook the chops under a preheated grill for about 7–8 minutes each side. Serve the chops with the rösti wedges and apple sauce.

Potato and Chicken Goulash

One Pot

I love making meals in one pot; it saves on the washing up.

Ingredients for 2

2 tbsp sunflower oil
2 chicken portions
1 small onion, peeled and
    cut into wedges
1 clove garlic, chopped
450g/1lb baby new potatoes,
    halved if large
1 tbsp plain flour
2 tsp paprika
150ml/¼pt chicken stock
2 tsp tomato purée
½ tsp dried mixed herbs
salt and freshly ground
    black pepper
crème fraîche to serve

Ingredients for 4

3 tbsp sunflower oil
4 chicken portions
1 large onion, peeled and
    cut into wedges
2 cloves garlic, chopped
900g/2lb baby new potatoes,
    halved if large
2 tbsp plain flour
1 tbsp paprika
300ml/½pt chicken stock
1 tbsp tomato purée
1 tsp dried mixed herbs
salt and freshly ground
    black pepper
crème fraîche to serve

1 Heat the oil in a large pan and fry the chicken quickly until browned on all sides. Remove from the pan.

2 Reduce the heat and stir in the onion, cook gently for 3–4 minutes until softened.

3 Add the garlic and potatoes to the pan.

4 Sprinkle with flour and paprika and cook, stirring, for 1 minute.

5 Stir in the stock, tomato purée and herbs. Season with salt and pepper.

6 Return the chicken to the pan. Cover and cook gently for 25–30 minutes until the potatoes are tender and the chicken is done.

7 Serve with a little crème fraîche spooned on top.

Sausage & Tomato Hotpot

Family Favourite

This is a filling dish that is good for midweek winter meals. You could replace the sausages with pieces of cod, in which case there is no need to pre-cook the fish; simply add it to the tomato–lentil mixture prior to layering up the dish.

Ingredients for 2

- **1 tbsp sunflower oil, plus extra for brushing**
- **4 good pork sausages**
- **1 onion, sliced**
- **½ tsp ground cumin**
- **400g/14oz can chopped tomatoes**
- **50g/2oz red split lentils**
- **150ml/¼pt chicken or beef stock**
- **500g/1lb 2oz medium potatoes, peeled**

Ingredients for 4

- **2 tbsp sunflower oil, plus extra for brushing**
- **8 good pork sausages**
- **1 large onion, sliced**
- **1 tsp ground cumin**
- **2 x 400g/14oz can chopped tomatoes**
- **100g/4oz red split lentils**
- **300ml/½pt chicken or beef stock**
- **1kg/2lb 4oz medium potatoes, peeled**

1 Heat the oil in a frying pan and add the sausages. Cook for about 10 minutes, turning frequently until browned and firm. Remove from the pan and cut into bite-size pieces.

2 Add the onion to the pan and cook for 3–4 minutes until soft. Stir in the cumin, tomatoes, lentils and stock, bring to the boil and simmer for 20 minutes.

3 Preheat the oven to 180°C/350°F/gas mark 4. Parboil the potatoes in boiling water for 5 minutes. Drain and allow to cool slightly. Slice the potatoes and arrange a layer at the bottom of a deep casserole dish.

4 Stir the sausage pieces into the tomato mixture.

5 Spoon on top of the potatoes.

6 Arrange a layer of potatoes on top. Brush the top with the oil.

7 Bake in the oven for 40–55 minutes, until the potato is tender and the top is golden.

Creamy Mushroom and Ham Bake

This is an economical family meal. Season lightly with salt as both the ham and cheese contain salt.

Ingredients for 2

450g/1lb medium floury
potatoes
75g/3oz button mushrooms,
sliced
75g/3oz sliced ham, cut
into strips
1 small onion, thinly sliced
75ml/2¹/₂fl oz milk
75g/3oz herb and garlic
cream cheese
15g/¹/₂oz butter
salt and freshly ground
black pepper

Ingredients for 4

900g/2lb medium floury
potatoes
175g/6oz button mushrooms,
sliced
175g/6oz sliced ham, cut
into strips
1 onion, thinly sliced
150ml/¹/₄pt milk
150g/5oz herb and garlic
cream cheese
25g/1oz butter
salt and freshly ground
black pepper

1 Preheat the oven to 180°C/350°F/gas mark 4. Grease a shallow ovenproof dish.

2 Parboil the potatoes in boiling water for 5 minutes. Drain and allow to cool slightly. Skin the potatoes and slice thinly. Arrange a layer in the bottom of the dish.

3 Add a layer of mushrooms, ham and onion.

4 Repeat the layers, finishing with a layer of potato. Lightly season the layers.

5 Heat the milk and cheese in a small pan, stirring until combined. Pour over the potatoes.

6 Dot the top with butter and bake for about 45 minutes, or until the potatoes are tender and the top is golden.

Sausages with Onion Gravy and Celeriac Mash

Comfort food at its best. The addition of celeriac to the mash gives a more sophisticated flavour, making this dish ideal for informal entertaining.

Ingredients for 2

15g/¹/₂oz butter
2 tsp olive oil
1 large onion, sliced
pinch dark brown sugar
1 tbsp plain flour
3 tbsp Madeira or red wine
**150ml/¹/₄pt good vegetable
    or beef stock**
**4 good-quality pork
    sausages**

Celeriac Mash

225g/8oz floury potatoes
225g/8oz celeriac
25g/1oz butter
splash of milk
**salt and freshly ground
    black pepper**

Ingredients for 4

25g/1oz butter
1 tbsp olive oil
2 large onions, sliced
¹/₄ tsp dark brown sugar
2 tbsp plain flour
**100ml/3¹/₂fl oz Madeira or red
    wine**
**300ml/¹/₂pt good vegetable
    or beef stock**
**8 good-quality pork
    sausages**

Celeriac Mash

450g/1lb floury potatoes
450g/1lb celeriac
50g/2oz butter
4 tbsp milk
**salt and freshly ground
    black pepper**

1 Heat the butter and oil in a saucepan and fry the onions over a low heat for 10 minutes until very soft.

2 Stir in the sugar and flour. Gradually add the Madeira or wine and then stir in the stock.

3 Bring to the boil, reduce the heat and simmer for 15 minutes.

4 Fry or grill the sausages for 15–20 minutes, turning frequently.

5 Meanwhile, peel and cut the potato and celeriac into 2.5cm/1in chunks. Cook

them in lightly salted boiling water for 10–12 minutes, or until just tender.

6 Drain well. Add the butter and milk and mash well. Season to taste.

7 Serve the mash with the sausages and onion gravy.

Perfect Fish and Chip Supper

Family Favourite

The key to good fish and chips is ensuring that the oil is at the correct temperature and that you do not crowd the pan too much.

Ingredients for 2

2 x 175g/6oz fillets of cod
  or haddock
100g/3½fl oz plain flour
1 tsp baking powder
½ tsp malt vinegar
about 100ml/4fl oz water
500g/1lb 2oz potatoes
oil for deep-frying
salt and freshly ground
  black pepper

Ingredients for 4

4 x 175g/6oz fillets of cod
  or haddock
200g/7oz plain flour
1 tsp baking powder
1 tsp malt vinegar
about 200ml/7fl oz water
1kg/2lb 4oz potatoes
oil for deep-frying
salt and freshly ground
  black pepper

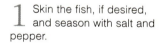

1 Skin the fish, if desired, and season with salt and pepper.

2 Make the batter by placing the flour and baking powder in a small bowl and making a well in the centre. Add the vinegar and gradually whisk in enough water to form a smooth, thick batter.

3 Peel and cut the potatoes into 1cm/½in thick chips.

4 Heat the oil in a deep-fat fryer or large saucepan to 180°C/350°F. (If using a saucepan do not fill more than one-third full.)

5 Add the chips and blanch for 5 minutes until just tender. You will need to do this in two batches if you are cooking for four people. Drain on kitchen paper and set aside.

6 Allow the temperature of the oil to come to 180–185°C/350–360°F. It may have dropped below this. Dip the fish into the batter and shake off excess.

7 Deep-fry the fish for 5–6 minutes until crisp and golden. Drain on kitchen paper and transfer to a warm serving plate. Keep warm.

8 Heat the oil again, this time to 190°C/375°F. Return the chips for 2-3 minutes until crisp and golden and piping hot. Again this is best done in two batches, if cooking for four people, to prevent the temperature of the oil dropping too much.

9 Drain well and serve with the fish.

Fish Pie

Family Favourite

This variation of a classic dish has a tasty topping of crunchy cubed potatoes rather than the more familiar mash. It is ideal for a midweek meal.

Ingredients for 2

175g/6oz cod or haddock fillet, skinned
175g/6oz smoked haddock fillet, skinned
300ml/¹/₂pt milk
40g/1¹/₂oz butter
1 leek, washed and sliced
25g/1oz plain flour
1 hard-boiled egg, cut into quarters
450g/1lb potatoes, peeled and cut into 1cm/¹/₂in cubes
salt and freshly ground black pepper

Ingredients for 4

350g/12oz cod or haddock fillet, skinned
350g/12oz smoked haddock fillet, skinned
600ml/1pt milk
75g/3oz butter
2 leeks, washed and sliced
50g/2oz plain flour
2 hard-boiled eggs, cut into quarters
900g/2lb potatoes, peeled and cut into 1cm/¹/₂in cubes
salt and freshly ground black pepper

1 Place the fish and milk in a saucepan. Cover and cook for 10 minutes, or until the fish flakes easily.

2 Remove the fish with a draining spoon. Strain the milk through a sieve and reserve. Flake the fish in large chunks.

3 Melt 25g/1oz (50g/2oz) butter in a saucepan and add the leek. Cook gently for 3 minutes, or until softened. Stir in the flour and cook for another minute.

4 Gradually stir in the milk and cook, stirring constantly, until the sauce thickens. Season to taste with salt and pepper.

5 Place the fish in an ovenproof dish and arrange the egg on top. Spoon the sauce over the fish.

6 Cook the potatoes in lightly salted boiling water for 5 minutes. Drain. Arrange on top of the egg.

7 Melt the remaining butter and brush over the top. Bake for 35–45 minutes at 200°C/400°F/gas mark 6 until the top is crisp and golden.

Barbequed Potato Skewers

Easy Entertaining

If you are using wooden skewers, soak them in cold water for at least 15 minutes to prevent them burning on the barbecue.

Ingredients for 2

12 baby new potatoes
150g/5oz thick loin cod
   steaks, skinned
6 slices pancetta or streaky
   bacon
grated zest 1/4 lemon
2 tsp lemon juice
1 tbsp olive oil
1 tsp honey
1 tsp wholegrain mustard
1 clove garlic, crushed
salt and freshly ground
   black pepper

Ingredients for 4

24 baby new potatoes
300g/10½oz thick loin cod
   steaks, skinned
12 slices pancetta or streaky
   bacon
grated zest ½ lemon
1 tbsp lemon juice
2 tbsp olive oil
1 tbsp honey
2 tsp wholegrain mustard
2 cloves garlic, crushed
salt and freshly ground
   black pepper

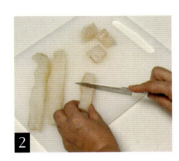

1 Cook the potatoes in boiling water for 12 minutes, or until only just tender when pierced with a skewer. Drain well.

2 Cut the cod into 12 (24) bite-size pieces. Cut the pancetta slices in half. If using streaky bacon, stretch the bacon with the back of a knife before cutting in half.

3 Wrap the pancetta or bacon around each piece of fish.

4 Whisk together the remaining ingredients to form a baste.

5 Thread the potatoes and wrapped cod pieces onto skewers. Brush the baste over the potatoes. Cook over hot barbecue coals, or under a grill, or on a hot griddle pan for 4–8 minutes, basting frequently.

Chunky Salmon and Potato Bake

One Pot

You can also make this dish with canned tuna; simply add chunks of the canned fish instead of the salmon steaks. If you like, a few chunks of fresh mozzarella cheese can also be scattered on top as soon as the dish leaves the oven. The residual heat will begin to melt the cheese – delicious!

Ingredients for 2

2 tbsp olive oil
350g/12oz new potatoes, halved or quartered if large
1 small red onion, cut into wedges
1/2 red pepper, seeded and cut into chunks
1/2 yellow pepper, seeded and cut into chunks
2 tomatoes, quartered
2 salmon steaks
lemon wedges to squeeze
salt and freshly ground black pepper

Ingredients for 4

4 tbsp olive oil
700g/1 1/2lb new potatoes, halved or quartered if large
1 red onion, cut into wedges
1 red pepper, seeded and cut into chunks
1 yellow pepper, seeded and cut into chunks
4 tomatoes, quartered
4 salmon steaks
lemon wedges to squeeze
salt and freshly ground black pepper

1 Preheat the oven to 200°C/400°F/gas Mark 6. Heat the oil in a roasting tin for about 3 minutes, add the potatoes, toss in the hot oil and roast for 30 minutes.

2 Add the onion, peppers and tomatoes and toss in the oil.

3 Arrange the salmon steaks on top. Season with salt and pepper. Roast for 15 minutes until the vegetables are tender and the fish is cooked.

4 Squeeze the lemon wedges over the top and serve immediately.

Salmon with Leek and Potato Pancakes

These leek and potato pancakes can also be served with grilled steak or chicken.

Ingredients for 2

15g/¹/₂oz butter
100g/4oz leeks, sliced
150g/5oz mashed potatoes
1 egg
25g/1oz plain flour
3 tbsp milk
olive oil
2 salmon fillets
1 tsp tomato purée
4 tbsp double cream
salt and freshly ground
**   black pepper**

Ingredients for 4

25g/1oz butter
225g/8oz leeks, sliced
250g/9oz mashed potatoes
2 eggs
50g/2oz plain flour
100ml/3¹/₂fl oz milk
olive oil
4 salmon fillets
2 tsp tomato purée
125ml/4floz double cream
salt and freshly ground
**   black pepper**

1 Melt the butter in a saucepan and sauté the leeks for 10 minutes until very soft.

2 Place the potato in a mixing bowl with the leeks. Beat in the eggs, flour and milk until well combined. Season with salt and pepper.

3 Heat a little oil in a heavy-based frying pan to grease the pan. Spoon two large tablespoonfuls of the mixture into the pan and spread to form a small round about 1cm/¹/₂in deep.

4 Cook for about 2 minutes until the underside is golden. Flip over and cook the other side.

5 Repeat with the remaining mixture until all the pancakes are made. Keep warm.

6 Heat 1–2 tablespoons of oil in a frying pan. Fry the salmon over a high heat for 3–4 minutes each side. Remove from the pan. Stir the tomato purée and cream into the pan and continue to stir until piping hot.

7 Serve the salmon on the leek pancakes with a little of the tomato sauce poured over the top.

Baked Tuna with Potatoes

Low Fat

I find this the perfect dish for a special occasion when time is short since it is very simple to prepare. To complete the meal, all you need is some fresh green vegetables or a crisp salad.

Ingredients for 2

350g/12oz small waxy
   potatoes
1 small red onion, sliced
   into thin wedges
1 tsp chopped fresh dill
2 tuna steaks about
   175g/6oz each
15g/¹/₂oz black or green
   olives
2 tbsp water
1 tbsp extra virgin olive oil
1 tsp lemon juice
salt and freshly ground
   black pepper
fresh dill to garnish

Ingredients for 4

700g/1¹/₂lb small waxy
   potatoes
1 red onion, sliced into
   thin wedges
1 tbsp chopped fresh dill
4 tuna steaks about
   175g/6oz each
25g/1oz black or green olives
4 tbsp water
2 tbsp extra virgin olive oil
1 tbsp lemon juice
salt and freshly ground
   black pepper
fresh dill to garnish

1 Preheat the oven to 200°C/400°F/gas mark 6. Lightly grease a shallow ovenproof dish. Blanch the potatoes in boiling water for 5–10 minutes until just tender. Drain. Allow to cool slightly and then slice thinly.

2 Arrange the potatoes and onion in one or two layers in the bottom of the dish and season with salt and pepper. Sprinkle with dill.

3 Arrange the tuna steaks on top and add the olives.

4 Drizzle the water, olive oil and lemon juice over the top. Bake for 20–25 minutes, or until the potatoes are tender.

Pan-fried Cod with Sweet Potato Mash

Easy Entertaining

Creamy mash with cod is a great combination.

Ingredients for 2

450g/1lb sweet potatoes, peeled
2 cod steaks
1 tbsp balsamic vinegar
1 tbsp sun-dried tomato purée
1 piece sun-dried tomato in oil, cut into strips
pinch sugar
75ml/2½fl oz fish stock
1 tbsp olive oil
50g/2oz cream cheese
salt and freshly ground black pepper

Ingredients for 4

900g/2lb sweet potatoes, peeled
4 cod steaks
2 tbsp balsamic vinegar
1 tbsp sun-dried tomato purée
2 pieces sun-dried tomatoes in oil, cut into strips
¼ tsp sugar
150ml/¼pt fish stock
2 tbsp olive oil
100g/4oz cream cheese
salt and freshly ground black pepper

1 Cut the potatoes into even-sized pieces of about 2cm/1in.

2 Place in a saucepan and add enough water to just cover the potatoes. Bring quickly to the boil and add a little salt. Reduce the heat and simmer for 10 minutes, or until just tender.

3 Meanwhile, season the fish with salt and pepper.

4 Place the vinegar, tomato purée, sun-dried tomato strips, sugar and fish stock in a small bowl and whisk together with a fork to make a vinaigrette sauce.

5 Heat the oil in a heavy-based frying pan and fry the fish for 3–4 minutes each side, until cooked. Keep warm.

6 Add the vinaigrette to the pan and stir to incorporate any juices in the pan. Take care because the liquid will splatter. Boil rapidly to reduce by half.

7 When the potatoes are cooked, drain well and return to the heat for a few seconds to drive off any remaining moisture.

8 Mash the potatoes well, add the cheese and continue to mash until smooth. Season with salt and pepper.

9 Pile the mash onto serving plates. Place the fish on top and drizzle over the dressing.

Vegetable Potato Pie

vegetarian

A great midweek family meal, this is a very versatile recipe. Use whatever vegetables you have to hand. You can even add cooked vegetables left over from another meal. If you like, you can add some chunks of fish to the sauce as well.

Ingredients for 2

1 carrot, thickly sliced
75g/3oz swede or pumpkin, cut into chunks
75g/3oz cauliflower florets
75g/3oz broccoli florets
25g/1oz frozen peas
25g/1oz frozen sweetcorn niblets
15g/1/2oz butter
15g/1/2oz flour
225ml/8fl oz milk
1 tsp Dijon mustard
350g/12oz floury potatoes, peeled
75g/3oz red Leicester cheese, grated
salt and freshly ground black pepper

Ingredients for 4

2 carrots, thickly sliced
175g/6oz swede or pumpkin, cut into chunks
175g/6oz cauliflower florets
175g/6oz broccoli florets
50g/2oz frozen peas
50g/2oz frozen sweetcorn niblets
25g/1oz butter
25g/1oz flour
450ml/3/4pt milk
1 tbsp Dijon mustard
700g/11/2lb floury potatoes, peeled
175g/6oz red Leicester cheese, grated
salt and freshly ground black pepper

1 Preheat the oven to 190°C/375°F/gas mark 5. Bring a pan of water to the boil and add the carrots and swede. Return to the boil and cook for 3 minutes.

2 Add the cauliflower and broccoli and cook for a further 3–5 minutes until the vegetables are just tender.

3 Add the peas and sweetcorn and remove from the heat. Drain and tip into a shallow ovenproof dish.

4 Melt the butter in a small saucepan and stir in the flour. Cook for 1 minute.

5 Remove from the heat and gradually beat in the milk. Return to the heat and cook, stirring constantly, until the sauce thickens slightly. Stir in the mustard and season with salt and pepper,

6 Pour the sauce over the vegetables and level the top.

7 Parboil the potatoes for 5 minutes. Drain and allow to cool slightly.

8 Grate the potatoes and toss with the cheese. Pile on top of the vegetables and bake for 45 minutes until the top is crisp and golden.

Potato, Spinach and Cheese Layer

vegetarian

This makes a great supper dish. Frozen spinach is very convenient but if you wish to use fresh spinach, double the quantity, cook until just wilted, drain and chop.

Ingredients for 2

- **1 tbsp olive oil, plus extra for brushing**
- **1 onion, chopped**
- **175g/6oz frozen spinach, thawed**
- **150g/5oz ricotta cheese**
- **100ml/3^1/$_2$fl oz milk**
- **450g/1lb medium waxy potatoes, peeled if desired**
- **1 tbsp fresh Parmesan cheese, grated**
- **salt and freshly ground black pepper**

Ingredients for 4

- **2 tbsp olive oil, plus extra for brushing**
- **1 large onion, chopped**
- **350g/12oz frozen spinach, thawed**
- **300g/10^1/$_2$oz ricotta cheese**
- **200ml/7fl oz milk**
- **900g/2lb medium waxy potatoes, peeled if desired**
- **2 tbsp fresh Parmesan cheese, grated**
- **salt and freshly ground black pepper**

1 Preheat the oven to 180°C/350°F/gas mark 4. Grease a shallow ovenproof dish.

2 Heat the oil and sauté the onion until softened. Remove from the heat.

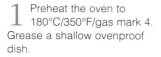

3 Chop the spinach and place in a mixing bowl. Beat in the ricotta cheese, milk and onion. Season well.

4 Parboil the potatoes in boiling water for 5 minutes. Drain and allow to cool slightly. Thinly slice the potatoes and arrange in a layer in the dish. Cover with a layer of the spinach mixture. Repeat layers, finishing with a layer of potato.

5 Brush the top with a little oil and sprinkle with Parmesan cheese.

6 Bake for about 45 minutes, or until the potatoes are tender and the top is golden.

Potato Ragu

Vegetarian

A simple vegetable stew. If you like, when not serving vegetarians, you can add chunks of ham.

Ingredients for 2

2 tbsp olive oil
225g/8oz carrots, sliced
225g/8oz new potatoes,
   sliced
1 leek, sliced
100g/4oz button mushrooms
150ml/¼pt vegetable stock
400g/14oz can chopped
   tomatoes with herbs
1 tsp cornflour
1 tbsp dry sherry
chopped fresh parsley to
   garnish, optional
salt and freshly ground
   black pepper

Ingredients for 4

4 tbsp olive oil
450g/1lb carrots, sliced
450g/1lb new potatoes,
   sliced
2 leeks, sliced
225g/8oz button mushrooms
300ml/½pt vegetable stock
2x 400g/14oz can chopped
   tomatoes with herbs
2 tsp cornflour
2 tbsp dry sherry
chopped fresh parsley to
   garnish, optional
salt and freshly ground
   black pepper

1 Heat the oil in a large saucepan and gently sauté the carrots, potatoes, leeks and mushrooms for 5 minutes until beginning to soften.

2 Add the stock and tomatoes. Bring to the boil, reduce the heat and simmer gently for 20–25 minutes.

3 Mix the cornflour and sherry together and stir into the pan. Cook, stirring, until thickened slightly.

4 Serve the ragu scattered with chopped fresh parsley.

on the side

Perfect Mash

Quick and Easy

No potato cookbook would be complete without a recipe for mash. Adding flavours to the mash makes for variety, and the combinations you can try are endless. I like a fairly firm mash but if you prefer a softer mash, increase the liquid until you have your required consistency. It is important that the milk is hot before being added. Many people have their preferred method of mashing potatoes. Purists would use a potato ricer, which forces the potato through small holes, but I prefer to use a hand-held potato masher. An electric whisk is very quick but take care not to over-beat or the mash will become glutinous. Maris Piper and King Edwards are ideal potato varieties for making mash.

Ingredients for 2

450g/1lb floury potatoes,
    peeled
25g/1oz butter
3–4 tbsp milk
salt and freshly ground
    black pepper
extra butter to serve

Ingredients for 4

900g/2lb floury potatoes,
    peeled
40g/1¹/₂oz butter
75–100ml/3–4fl oz milk
salt and freshly ground
    black pepper
extra butter to serve

Flavourings (optional):

Wholegrain mustard, pesto, horseradish sauce or harissa paste.

1 Cut the potatoes into pieces of about 2cm/1in. Rinse under cold water to remove excess starch.

2 Place in a saucepan and add enough water to just cover the potatoes. Bring quickly to the boil and add a little salt. Reduce the heat and simmer for 10 minutes, or until just tender. Test with a skewer.

3 Meanwhile, heat the milk until almost boiling. Drain the potatoes and return to the heat for a few seconds to drive off any remaining moisture.

4 Mash the potatoes, add the butter and hot milk and continue to mash until smooth.

5 Season. Beat in any flavouring, if using. Add a little at a time until you have the desired intensity of flavour. Transfer to a serving bowl with a little extra butter.

Crumb-topped Mash

I just love garlic with potatoes; the two flavours complement each other perfectly. In this dish, there is the delicious attraction of a fabulous crunchy topping with the creamy mash.

Ingredients for 2

400g/14oz floury potatoes, peeled and cut into small chunks
25g/1oz butter
3 tbsp milk
salt and freshly ground black pepper

Topping

3 tbsp olive oil
1 to 2 cloves garlic, chopped
40g/1½oz fresh breadcrumbs
2 tbsp chopped fresh parsley

Ingredients for 4

800g/1lb 12oz floury potatoes, peeled and cut into small chunks
40g/1½oz butter
6 tbsp milk
salt and freshly ground black pepper

Topping

6 tbsp olive oil
3 cloves garlic, chopped
75g/3oz fresh breadcrumbs
4 tbsp chopped fresh parsley

1 Place the potatoes in a saucepan and cover with water. Bring quickly to the boil, reduce the heat and simmer for 10–12 minutes, or until tender.

2 Preheat the oven to 200°C/400°F/gas mark 6. Lightly grease a shallow ovenproof dish.

3 Meanwhile, heat the butter and milk together in a small pan until the butter has melted and the milk is almost boiling.

4 Drain the potatoes and return to the heat briefly to evaporate any liquid. Pour the hot milk over the potatoes and mash until smooth. Season with salt and pepper.

5 To make the topping, heat the oil in a frying pan. Stir in the garlic and sauté for 1 minute. Stir in the breadcrumbs and remove from the heat. Stir in the parsley.

6 Pile the potato into the prepared dish and spread the topping over it. Bake in the oven for 15–20 minutes until the topping is crisp and golden.

Leek and Bacon Mash

Easy Entertaining

This mash is perfect served with grilled fish. For simple, formal entertaining, pile the mash in the centre of the plate, top with the fish and drizzle a little balsamic vinegar and olive oil over the top.

Ingredients for 2

**350g/12oz medium floury
    potatoes, peeled**
1oz/25g butter
**1 large leek, sliced and
    washed well**
**3 rashers smoked streaky
    bacon, chopped**
75ml/2¹/₂fl oz milk
**salt and freshly ground
    black pepper**
**generous pinch grated
    nutmeg**

Ingredients for 4

**700g/1¹/₂lb medium floury
    potatoes, peeled**
2oz/50g butter
**2 large leeks, sliced and
    washed well**
**6 rashers smoked streaky
    bacon, chopped**
150ml/¹/₄ pt milk
**salt and freshly ground
    black pepper**
**generous pinch grated
    nutmeg**

1 Cut the potatoes into even-sized pieces. Place in a saucepan and add enough water to cover. Bring quickly to the boil.

2 Reduce the heat, cover and simmer for 12–15 minutes, or until tender when pierced with a skewer. Drain.

3 In a separate pan, melt the butter and sauté the leek and bacon for 5–10 minutes until softened.

4 Add the milk and bring to a gentle simmer. Remove from the heat and keep warm.

5 Mash the potatoes until smooth. Season with salt, pepper and nutmeg. Add the leek and bacon mixture and mix well. Serve immediately.

Mixed Root Mash

Family Favourite

This dish has been a favourite of mine since the children were toddlers. It has a slightly sweet flavour that is popular with children.

Ingredients for 2

200g/7oz floury potatoes, peeled
100g/4oz sweet potatoes, peeled
100g/4oz parsnips, peeled
1 small carrot, peeled
2 tbsp olive oil
salt and freshly ground black pepper

Ingredients for 4

400g/14oz floury potatoes, peeled
200g/7oz sweet potatoes, peeled
200g/7oz parsnips, peeled
1 large carrot, peeled
4 tbsp olive oil
salt and freshly ground black pepper

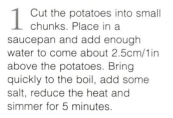

1 Cut the potatoes into small chunks. Place in a saucepan and add enough water to come about 2.5cm/1in above the potatoes. Bring quickly to the boil, add some salt, reduce the heat and simmer for 5 minutes.

2 Cut the other vegetables into small chunks.

3 Add to the pan and return to the boil, then cover and simmer for 5–6 minutes, or until all the vegetables are tender.

4 Drain, reserving a little of the cooking liquid. Add half the olive oil and mash until smooth. Beat in a few tablespoons of the cooking liquid. The mash should not be too wet and it should also have a mixture of textures, from the creamy potato to the chunky carrot and more fibrous parsnip.

5 Season with freshly ground black pepper. Pile the potato into a serving dish and drizzle over the remaining olive oil.

Duchesse Potatoes

Freezer Friendly

This classic dish is ideal when you need to prepare a dish in advance. Once made, it can be kept in the refrigerator and baked when required. I have given the dish a new twist with the addition of a little chilli and coriander, but you can leave the potato plain if you prefer. It is very important that the potato is smooth, or the piping will be difficult. Press through a nylon sieve if required.

Freeze for up to 3 months. Cook from frozen, allowing an extra 5–10 minutes cooking time.

Ingredients for 2

350g/12oz floury potatoes
25g/1oz butter
1 small egg
1 tsp chilli purée
1 tbsp finely chopped coriander
beaten egg to glaze
salt

Ingredients for 4

700g/1½lb floury potatoes
50g/2oz butter
1 egg
2 tsp chilli purée
2 tbsp finely chopped coriander
beaten egg to glaze
salt

1 Peel the potatoes and cut into equal-size pieces. Place the potatoes in a saucepan and cover with water. Bring quickly to the boil, lightly salt the water, reduce the heat and simmer for 10–15 minutes, depending on the size of the pieces, until just tender.

2 Preheat the oven to 200°C/400°F/gas mark 6. Lightly grease one or two baking sheets.

3 Drain the potatoes and return the pan to the heat briefly to evaporate any liquid. Add the butter and mash until smooth.

4 Beat in the egg, chilli purée and coriander.

5 Pipe rosettes onto the prepared baking sheet. Add a splash of water to the beaten egg and carefully brush each rosette with beaten egg. Bake for 25 minutes until golden brown.

Potato Croquettes

Family Favourite

Perfect for using leftover potato, these will be popular with young and old alike. I like the extra flavour the harissa paste gives the mash but it can be omitted, if preferred.

Ingredients for 2

350g/12oz cooked potatoes,
  mashed
4 spring onions, finely
  sliced
2 tsp harissa paste (optional)
2 tbsp chopped fresh parsley
1 small egg, beaten
40g/1¹/₂oz dried breadcrumbs
4 tbsp olive oil
salt and freshly ground
  black pepper
fresh parsley to garnish

Ingredients for 4

700g/1¹/₂lb cooked potatoes,
  mashed
bunch spring onions, finely
  sliced
1 tbsp harissa paste
  (optional)
4 tbsp chopped fresh parsley
1 egg, beaten
75g/3oz dried breadcrumbs
6 to 8 tbsp olive oil
salt and freshly ground
  black pepper
fresh parsley to garnish

1 Place the mashed potato in a bowl with the spring onion and harissa paste, if using.

2 Add the parsley, season to taste and mix well.

3 Divide into 4 (8) equal portions and shape into logs.

4 Dip each log in beaten egg and coat with breadcrumbs.

5 Heat the oil in a heavy-based frying pan and fry for 8–10 minutes, turning frequently until crisp and golden. Garnish with parsley.

Perfect Roast Potatoes

Family Favourite

Crisp on the outside, fluffy on the inside. Goose fat is my preferred fat for roast potatoes as it gives a crisp finish and a great flavour. You can buy it in delis and larger supermarkets. Choose medium-sized potatoes and cut into three or four pieces. Maris pipers are my favourite variety for roast potatoes.

Ingredients for 2

450g/1lb floury potatoes
4 tbsp goose fat, lard or
**   sunflower oil**
sea salt, preferably Maldon
coarsely ground black
**   pepper**

Ingredients for 4

900g/2lb floury potatoes
8 tbsp goose fat, lard or
**   sunflower oil**
sea salt, preferably Maldon
coarsely ground black
**   pepper**

1 Preheat the oven to 200°C/400°F/gas mark 6.

2 Peel and cut the potatoes so that all the pieces are about the same size.

3 Place in a saucepan of lightly salted water, cover and bring quickly to the boil.

4 Reduce the heat and simmer gently for 5 minutes.

5 Meanwhile, place the fat in a shallow-sided roasting tin and heat in the oven.

6 Drain the potatoes and return to the pan. Put the lid on the pan. Holding it in place, shake the pan up and down a few times. This will fluff up the outsides of the potatoes.

7 Tip the potatoes onto the tray and turn to coat in the hot fat.

8 Roast for 50–60 minutes, turning the potatoes once or twice during the cooking time. Serve immediately, sprinkled with salt and pepper.

Roasted Rosemary Potatoes with Garlic

Easy Entertaining

These roasted potatoes have a fabulous flavour, which goes well with roast meats.

Ingredients for 2

450g/1lb floury potatoes, peeled
3 tbsp olive or sunflower oil
1 tbsp chopped fresh rosemary
1 clove garlic, chopped
salt

Ingredients for 4

900g/2lb floury potatoes, peeled
5 tbsp olive or sunflower oil
2 tbsp chopped fresh rosemary
2 cloves garlic, chopped
salt

1 Preheat the oven to 200°C/400°F/gas mark 6.

2 Choose medium potatoes and cut into two or three pieces.

3 Pour the oil into a shallow roasting tin. Place in the oven to heat for 5 minutes.

4 Remove the tray from the oven. Add the potatoes and sprinkle with rosemary. Turn the potatoes so that they are coated in the hot oil and return to the oven.

5 Roast for 30 minutes, sprinkle over the chopped garlic, then turn and baste the potatoes in the oil.

6 Roast for a further 20–30 minutes until crisp and golden, turning and basting in the oil once more during cooking.

7 Serve immediately, sprinkled with salt.

Smashed Potatoes with Coriander Pesto

Freezer Friendly

Not quite a mash, this potato dish is packed with lots of texture and flavours that have an oriental twist. The pesto is fiddly to make in a small quantity so make up one batch and keep in the refrigerator for up to 4 days. The pesto can also be served with fish or tossed into pasta or Chinese noodles. Freeze for up to 2 months and allow to defrost completely before reheating.

Ingredients for 2

450g/1lb new potatoes
2 tbsp coriander pesto
salt

Ingredients for 4

900g/2lb new potatoes
4 tbsp coriander pesto
salt

Coriander pesto:

50g/2oz coriander leaves
50g/2oz cashew nuts
2 green chillies, seeded and chopped
1 tsp ground coriander
2 tbsp white wine vinegar
1 tbsp lime juice
1 tbsp sunflower oil
1 tbsp natural yoghurt

1 Place the potatoes in a saucepan with just enough water to cover. Bring to the boil and salt the water if desired.

2 Cover with a well-fitting lid and simmer gently for 20–25 minutes until just tender when pierced with a skewer.

3 Meanwhile, make the coriander pesto. Place all the ingredients into a food processor and process to form a coarse paste.

4 Drain the potatoes well and return to the heat briefly to drive off any moisture.

5 Allow to cool slightly and peel half to three-quarters of the potatoes.

6 Smash the peeled potatoes with a large fork to roughly mash.

7 Add the pesto and unpeeled potatoes and break these up lightly with the fork. The potatoes should not be completely mashed but retain some chunky texture, mixed with the smoother creamed potato.

8 If the potatoes have become too cold, place in an oiled dish and reheat in the oven at 190°C/375°F/gas mark 5 for 15–20 minutes before serving.

Spiced Roast Potatoes

I always have a jar of curry paste on the shelf because it is perfect for adding extra flavour to the simplest of dishes.

Ingredients for 2

350g/12oz floury potatoes
1 tbsp mild or medium curry paste
2 tbsp sunflower oil

Ingredients for 4

700g/1½lb floury potatoes
2 tbsp mild or medium curry paste
4 tbsp sunflower oil

1 Preheat the oven to 200°C/400°F/gas mark 6.

2 Peel and cut the potatoes so that all the pieces are about the same size, 5cm/2in is ideal.

3 Place in a saucepan of lightly salted water, cover and bring quickly to the boil.

4 Reduce the heat and simmer gently for 5 minutes.

5 Meanwhile, combine the curry paste and oil.

6 Drain the potatoes and return to the pan. Pour the oil and curry paste over the potatoes.

7 Put the lid on the pan, hold it in place and shake the pan up and down a few times. This will fluff up the outsides of the potatoes.

8 Tip the potatoes into a shallow roasting tin.

9 Roast for 40–60 minutes, depending on the size of the pieces. Turn the potatoes once or twice during the cooking time. Serve immediately.

Crushed Roast Potatoes with Olive and Sun-dried Tomato Dressing

Tossed in a piquant dressing, these potatoes are fabulous served with barbecued or plain grilled meat and fish. Crushing the potatoes means that some of the flavour is absorbed into the potato itself.

Ingredients for 2

450g/1lb baby new potatoes
4 tbsp extra virgin olive oil
1/2 red onion, roughly
    chopped
4 sun-dried tomatoes
4 pitted black olives,
    chopped
a small handful flat-leaved
    parsley
1 tbsp red wine vinegar
salt and freshly ground
    black pepper

Ingredients for 4

900g/2lb baby new potatoes
6 tbsp extra virgin olive oil
1 small red onion, roughly
    chopped
8 sun-dried tomatoes
8 pitted black olives,
    chopped
a large handful flat-leaved
    parsley
2 tbsp red wine vinegar
salt and freshly ground
    black pepper

1 Preheat the oven to 200°C/400°F/gas 6.

2 Place the potatoes in a roasting tin and drizzle with 2 tbsp (3 tbsp) of the oil.

3 Sprinkle with a little salt and roast for 30 minutes, turning occasionally until tender.

4 Meanwhile, place the remaining oil, onion, tomatoes, olives, parsley and vinegar in a food processor and chop finely.

5 Lightly crush each potato with a fork and then toss in the onion and parsley mixture. Serve immediately.

Sautéed Potatoes with Golden Pine Nuts

Easy Entertaining

Sautéed potatoes are given extra flavour with a few simple additions.

Ingredients for 2

**350g/12oz small new
    potatoes
3 tbsp olive oil
2 tbsp pine nuts
1 clove garlic, chopped
salt and freshly ground black
    pepper**

Ingredients for 4

**700g/1½lb small new
    potatoes
6 tbsp olive oil
4 tbsp pine nuts
2 cloves garlic, chopped
salt and freshly ground black
    pepper**

1 Place the potatoes in a large saucepan and cover with water. Bring to the boil and simmer for 10 minutes.

2 Drain and allow to cool slightly until cool enough to handle.

3 Peel and cut the potatoes into quarters or bite-size pieces.

4 Heat the oil in a large frying pan, add the pine nuts and cook until pale golden. Remove with a draining spoon and set aside.

5 Add the potatoes and sauté until pale golden.

6 Add the garlic and continue to sauté until the potatoes are crisp and golden.

7 Transfer to a warm serving dish, season with salt and pepper and sprinkle with the pine nuts. Serve immediately.

Sesame Sautéed Potatoes

This side dish is good enough to make from scratch but it is also a great way of using up leftover boiled potatoes, starting from step 3.

Ingredients for 2

350g/12oz waxy potatoes
2 tbsp olive oil
1 tbsp sesame oil
1 tbsp sesame seeds
salt and freshly ground
    black pepper

Ingredients for 4

700g/1½lb waxy potatoes
4 tbsp olive oil
2 tbsp sesame oil
2 tbsp sesame seeds
salt and freshly ground
    black pepper

1 Place the potatoes in a large saucepan and cover with water. Bring to the boil and simmer for 10 minutes.

2 Drain and allow to cool slightly until cool enough to handle.

3 Peel and cut the potatoes into thick slices. Heat the oils in a large non-stick frying pan. Ideally, the pan should be large enough to take all the potatoes in one layer.

4 Add the potatoes to the pan and cook over a medium-high heat for 5 minutes until beginning to crisp.

5 Turn the potatoes over with a fish slice or draining spoon and cook for a further 5–10 minutes until crisp on all sides.

6 When the potatoes are almost cooked, add the sesame seeds to the pan and toss with the potatoes for the last few minutes of cooking until they too are pale golden.

7 Serve sprinkled with salt and pepper

Curried Potatoes with Thai Spices

Perfect for using leftover potatoes, this side dish goes well with grilled chicken.

Ingredients for 2

350g/12oz cooked potatoes
2 tbsp olive oil
1 tbsp Thai red curry paste
2 tsp water
coriander leaves to garnish

Ingredients for 4

700g/1½lb cooked potatoes
4 tbsp olive oil
2 tbsp Thai red curry paste
1 tbsp water
coriander leaves to garnish

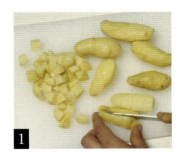

1 Cut the potatoes into dice. Heat the oil in a large non-stick frying pan. Ideally the pan should be large enough to take all the potatoes in one layer.

2 Add the potatoes to the pan and cook over a medium-high heat for 5 minutes until beginning to crisp.

3 Turn the potatoes over with a fish slice or draining spoon and cook for a further 5 minutes.

4 Mix the curry paste with the water. Stir into the pan and continue to cook for a further 1–2 minutes until the potatoes are crisp on all sides.

5 Serve sprinkled with coriander leaves.

Gratin Dauphinois

Easy Entertaining

A classic French dish from the mountainous Dauphine region. There are two schools of thought: those who make the dish with the addition of grated cheese on top, and those who claim the true gratin Dauphinois does not contain cheese. So the choice is up to you!

Ingredients for 2

knob of butter
200ml/7fl oz double cream
75ml/2½fl oz milk
1 clove garlic, crushed
450g/1lb floury potatoes,
    peeled
25g/1oz Emmenthal cheese,
    grated (optional)
25g/1oz Gruyère cheese
    grated (optional)
salt and freshly ground
    black pepper

Ingredients for 4

15g/½oz butter
400ml/14fl oz double cream
150ml/¼pt milk
2 cloves garlic, crushed
900g/2lb floury potatoes,
    peeled
50g/2oz Emmenthal cheese,
    grated (optional)
50g/2oz Gruyère cheese,
    grated (optional)
salt and freshly ground
    black pepper

1 Preheat the oven to 170°C/325°F/gas mark 3. Generously grease a shallow, ovenproof dish with some of the butter.

2 Place the cream and milk in a saucepan with the garlic, and heat until just simmering. Remove from the heat. Season well with salt and pepper.

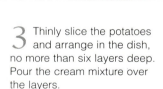

3 Thinly slice the potatoes and arrange in the dish, no more than six layers deep. Pour the cream mixture over the layers.

4 Mix together the cheeses, if using, and sprinkle over the top of the dish. Dot with any remaining butter.

5 Bake for about 1½ hours, or until the potatoes are tender and the top is golden.

Jansson's Temptation

A classic Swedish dish that goes well with both meat and fish dishes. Do not add extra salt as the anchovies add enough saltiness to the dish for most peoples' tastes.

Ingredients for 2

25g/1oz butter
1 onion, sliced
40g/1¹/₂oz can anchovy fillets, chopped
500g/1lb 2oz waxy potatoes, cut into thin sticks
100ml/3¹/₂fl oz cream
freshly ground black pepper

Ingredients for 4

40g/1¹/₂oz butter
2 onions, sliced
75g/3oz can anchovies, chopped
1kg/2¹/₄lb waxy potatoes, cut into sticks
200ml/7fl oz single cream
freshly ground black pepper

1 Preheat the oven to 190°C/375°F/gas mark 5. Grease a shallow, ovenproof dish.

2 Melt half the butter in a frying pan and fry the onion for about 10 minutes until softened and just beginning to caramelise. Stir in the anchovies.

3 Spread half the potatoes in a layer in the dish and top with the onion mixture.

4 Spread the remaining potato on top.

5 Pour the cream over the potatoes and dot with the remaining butter.

6 Bake in the oven for 50–60 minutes until the potatoes are tender and the top golden.

Cheesy Potato Bake

Grated potato and cheese are baked together for this fabulous side dish with a great crispy topping.

Ingredients for 2

1 tbsp sunflower oil
¹/₂ onion, chopped
1 clove garlic, chopped
575g/1¹/₄lb potatoes
**100g/4oz Emmenthal cheese,
  grated**
**225ml/8fl oz hot chicken or
  vegetable stock**
15g/¹/₂oz breadcrumbs
15g/¹/₂oz rolled oats
**salt and freshly ground
  black pepper**

Ingredients for 4

2 tbsp sunflower oil
1 onion, chopped
2 cloves garlic, chopped
1.1kg/2¹/₂lb potatoes
**200g/7oz Emmenthal cheese,
  grated**
**450ml/³/₄pt hot chicken or
  vegetable stock**
40g/1¹/₂oz breadcrumbs
40g/1¹/₂oz rolled oats
**salt and freshly ground
  black pepper**

1 Preheat the oven to 190°C/375°F/gas mark 5. Lightly grease a shallow baking dish.

2 Heat the oil in a frying pan and sauté the onion for 5 minutes until softened and beginning to colour. Add the garlic and sauté for 1 minute.

3 Peel and coarsely grate the potatoes. Spread one-third of the potatoes in a layer in the prepared dish. Top with one-third of the cheese. Season with salt and pepper.

4 Repeat the layers and then spread the final portion of potato on top.

5 Pour stock over the potatoes.

6 Mix the remaining cheese with the breadcrumbs and oats. Sprinkle on top of the potato and bake for 45 minutes, or until the potatoes are tender.

Herby Potato Stacks

Easy Entertaining

A simple and attractive way to serve potatoes as an accompaniment. You can vary the herb mix to your own preference.

Ingredients for 2

350g/12oz floury potatoes
25g/1oz melted butter
¹/₂ tsp chopped fresh
**   rosemary**
¹/₂ tsp chopped fresh thyme
¹/₂ tsp chopped fresh sage
2 tsp chopped fresh parsley
salt and freshly ground
**   black pepper**

Ingredients for 4

700g/1¹/₂lb floury potatoes
50g/2oz melted butter
1 tsp chopped fresh
**   rosemary**
1 tsp chopped fresh thyme
1 tsp chopped fresh sage
1 tbsp chopped fresh parsley
salt and freshly ground
**   black pepper**

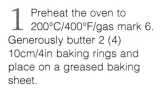

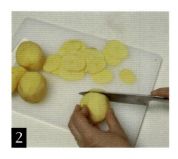

1 Preheat the oven to 200°C/400°F/gas mark 6. Generously butter 2 (4) 10cm/4in baking rings and place on a greased baking sheet.

2 Slice the potatoes very thinly about 1mm/¹/₁₆in thick.

3 Toss the herbs together with the salt and pepper to mix.

4 Arrange the potato slices in layers inside the rings. Drizzle with a little melted butter and sprinkle each layer with the herb mixture.

5 Continue layering the potatoes, finishing with a layer of potato. Drizzle butter over the top.

6 Bake for 35–40 minutes until tender and the tops are golden. Press the potato down a few times during the cooking to form a solid cake.

7 To serve, carefully remove the baking rings and transfer the stack of potato to a warm serving plate.

Foil-baked Potatoes in a Sesame Dressing

I first tasted this dressing while on holiday in Australia, where it was served on a green salad. I felt the flavours would also go well with potatoes, so back home I gave it a try and I was right. I hope you agree.

Ingredients for 2

350g/12oz baby potatoes, washed
1 tsp sesame seeds
2 tbsp sesame oil
2 spring onions, shredded
½ small chilli, seeded and shredded
1 tbsp soy sauce
2 tsp white wine vinegar

Ingredients for 4

700g/1½lb baby potatoes, washed
2 tsp sesame seeds
4 tbsp sesame oil
4 spring onions, shredded
1 small chilli, seeded and shredded
2 tbsp soy sauce
1 tbsp white wine vinegar

1 Preheat the oven to 190°C/375°F/gas mark 5. Divide the potatoes equally between 2 (4) large squares of foil.

2 Place the sesame seeds in a heavy-based pan and heat until the seeds are golden, shaking the pan frequently.

3 Pour in the sesame oil, swirl it around the hot pan and remove the pan from the heat.

4 Stir in the remaining dressing ingredients. Spoon equally over the potatoes and fold up the foil to form parcels that completely enclose the potatoes.

5 Place on a baking sheet and bake for 40–45 minutes, or until the potatoes are tender. Serve in the foil.

Chunky Herbed Oven Chips

Low Fat

With much less fat than fried chips these chips can become a regular treat. I love the crunch of the flakes of Maldon salt on chips. There is no need to grind the salt, just sprinkle a little over the chips.

Ingredients for 2

250g/9oz medium floury potatoes, cut into wedges
2 tbsp olive oil
1/4 tsp dried rosemary
1/4 tsp dried thyme
generous pinch dried sage
sea salt, preferably Maldon

Ingredients for 4

500g/1lb 2oz medium floury potatoes, cut into wedges
3 tbsp olive oil
1/2 tsp dried rosemary
1/2 tsp dried thyme
1/4 tsp dried sage
sea salt, preferably Maldon

1 Preheat the oven to 200°C/400°F/gas mark 6.

2 Place the potatoes in a bowl of water for 10 minutes to remove excess starch. Drain well and pat dry with kitchen paper or a clean tea towel.

3 Put the potatoes, oil and herbs in a large bowl and toss together until well coated.

4 Spread out on a baking sheet in a single layer.

5 Bake in the centre of the oven for 30–40 minutes, turning once or twice to ensure even browning.

6 When tender and golden, sprinkle with salt and serve immediately.

Spicy Oven Chips with Onion Wedges

Family Favourite

Liven up everyday meals with these spicy oven-baked chips.

Ingredients for 2

350g/12oz potatoes
1 red onion
2 cloves garlic, peeled and halved
1 tbsp lemon juice
1 tbsp water
2 tsp tomato purée
2 tbsp olive oil
1/2 tsp dried mixed herbs
1 tsp paprika
1/2 tsp chilli powder
salt and freshly ground black pepper

Ingredients for 4

700g/11/2lb potatoes
2 red onions
4 cloves garlic, peeled and halved
2 tbsp lemon juice
2 tbsp water
1 tbsp tomato purée
4 tbsp olive oil
1 tsp dried mixed herbs
2 tsp paprika
1 tsp chilli powder
salt and freshly ground black pepper

1 Preheat the oven to 200°C/400°F/gas mark 6.

2 Peel and cut the potatoes into chunky chips.

3 Peel the onions and cut into wedges.

4 Toss the potato chips, garlic and onion together in a large bowl.

5 Place the lemon juice, water, tomato purée and oil in a small bowl and whisk together with a fork.

6 Stir in the herbs and spices. Drizzle over the potato and onion mixture and toss together to coat well. Season with salt and pepper.

7 Spread out in a single layer on a baking sheet.

8 Bake for 40–50 minutes until the potatoes are tender.

Microwave Potato Wedges with Cheese and Chilli

Quick and Easy

Knock up this spicy potato dish in minutes, using just a few store cupboard standbys.

Ingredients for 2

**2 medium potatoes,
    scrubbed (about
    350g/12oz)**
2 tbsp water
1 tbsp olive oil
1 tsp chilli purée
**1 red chilli, seeded and thinly
    sliced (optional)**
50g/2oz cheese, grated

Ingredients for 4

**4 medium potatoes,
    scrubbed (about
    700g/1½lb)**
4 tbsp water
2 tbsp olive oil
1 tbsp chilli purée
**1 red chilli, seeded and thinly
    sliced (optional)**
100g/4oz cheese, grated

1 Cut each potato into eight wedges. Place the potato wedges in a microwave-proof dish.

2 Add the water. Cover with cling wrap, leaving a space for the steam to escape, and cook on full power for approximately 8–10 minutes for 2 servings and 12–15 minutes for 4 servings, Stir twice during the cooking time.

3 Drain the potatoes.

4 Mix together the oil, chilli purée and chilli slices, if using, in a bowl. Pour over the potatoes and toss the potatoes in the mixture.

5 Pile into a flameproof dish and sprinkle with the cheese. Place under a hot grill for 2 minutes until the cheese melts.

Cooks tip:
Use whatever cheese you have to hand: Cheddar, Gruyère and Emmenthal all work well.

New Potatoes with Minted Peas & Pancetta

Serve this dish with plain grilled meat or chicken for a complete meal.

Ingredients for 2

250g/9oz baby new potatoes, washed
175g/6oz frozen peas
1 tbsp olive oil
50g/2oz diced pancetta
4 spring onions, sliced
4 tbsp reduced-fat crème fraîche
1 tbsp chopped fresh mint
salt and freshly ground black pepper
fresh mint to garnish

Ingredients for 4

500g/1lb 2oz baby new potatoes washed
350g/12oz frozen peas
2 tbsp olive oil
100g/4oz diced pancetta
8 spring onions, sliced
125g/4¹/₂oz reduced-fat crème fraîche
2 tbsp chopped fresh mint
salt and freshly ground black pepper
fresh mint to garnish

1 Bring a large saucepan of water to the boil and add the potatoes. Bring the water back to boiling over a high heat and simmer for 12 minutes until the potatoes are almost tender.

2 Add the peas and return to the boil to simmer for 2– minutes.

3 Meanwhile, heat the olive oil in a frying pan and sauté the pancetta until beginning to brown. Add the spring onions and sauté until just softened.

4 Stir in the crème fraîche and mint.

5 When the potatoes and peas are cooked, drain and add to the frying pan.

6 Toss until coated in the sauce, season to taste and garnish with mint. Serve immediately.

Orange Glazed New Potatoes

A simple glaze gives new potatoes a tasty twist.

Ingredients for 2

**350g/12oz small new
  potatoes**
15g/¹/₂oz butter
¹/₂ tsp grated orange zest
2 tbsp orange juice
**1 tbsp light muscovado
  sugar**
¹/₄ tsp ground cumin
**about 4 basil leaves,
  shredded**
**salt and freshly ground
  black pepper**
basil leaves to garnish

Ingredients for 4

**700g/1¹/₂lb small new
  potatoes**
25g/1oz butter
1 tsp grated orange zest
4 tbsp orange juice
**2 tbsp light muscovado
  sugar**
¹/₂ tsp ground cumin
**about 4 basil leaves,
  shredded**
**salt and freshly ground
  black pepper**
basil leaves to garnish

1 Place the potatoes in a saucepan with just enough water to cover. Bring to the boil, reduce heat, cover and simmer for 15–20 minutes until tender.

2 Drain, return to the pan and keep warm.

3 Melt the butter in a small pan and stir in the orange zest, juice, sugar and cumin.

4 Pour the orange glaze over the potatoes. Add the shredded basil and toss to coat well. Pile into a serving dish and serve garnished with basil leaves.

New Potatoes with Oregano and Lemon Butter

This quantity of butter will serve about 6 to 8 people. It is fiddly to make up a small quantity of the butter, so any remaining butter can be stored in the refrigerator for up to 2 weeks and in the freezer for up to 1 month. A salad or speciality potato is ideal for this recipe: try pink fir apples for extra flavour.

Ingredients for 2

350g/12oz salad or speciality
   potatoes
about 40g/1½oz oregano
   and lemon butter
salt

Ingredients for 4

700g/1½lb salad or speciality
   potatoes
about 75g/3oz oregano
   and lemon butter
salt

Oregano and lemon butter:

100g/4oz butter, softened
1 tsp dried oregano or
   1 tbsp chopped fresh oregano
grated zest and juice ½ lemon
salt and freshly ground black pepper

1 To make the butter, beat together all the ingredients. Chill until required.

2 Bring a large saucepan of water to the boil, salt the water and add the potatoes.

3 Return the water to the boil, reduce the heat, cover the pan and simmer for 15–20 minutes until just tender.

4 When the potatoes are cooked, drain and transfer to a warm serving dish.

5 Place two or three generous knobs of butter on top and toss before serving, so that the butter melts and the potatoes are lightly coated in the butter.

Potatoes in Mojo Sauce

The recipe for this mojo sauce originates in the Canary Islands. The potatoes can be served as a side dish with grilled fish or as a Spanish tapas dish. Choose a potato that will not break up when boiling.

Ingredients for 2

- 1/2 **red chilli pepper**
- **2 tomatoes**
- **350g/12oz baby new potatoes**
- **4 cloves garlic**
- **1/2 tsp cumin**
- **2 tbsp extra virgin olive oil**
- **1 tbsp red wine vinegar**
- **1 tbsp water**
- **salt**

Ingredients for 4

- **1 red chilli pepper**
- **4 tomatoes**
- **700g/11/2lb baby new potatoes**
- **8 cloves garlic**
- **1 tsp cumin**
- **4 tbsp extra virgin olive oil**
- **2 tbsp red wine vinegar**
- **2 tbsp water**
- **salt**

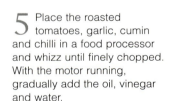

1 Preheat the oven to 180°C/350°F/gas mark 5.

2 Cut the chilli in half and remove the seeds. Roughly chop.

3 Cut the tomatoes in half, scoop out the seeds and discard them. Place the tomato halves on a lightly oiled baking sheet and roast for 30 minutes.

4 Cook the potatoes in lightly salted boiling water for 12–15 minutes, or until just tender.

5 Place the roasted tomatoes, garlic, cumin and chilli in a food processor and whizz until finely chopped. With the motor running, gradually add the oil, vinegar and water.

6 Drain the potatoes and transfer to a warm serving plate. Pour the mojo sauce over the potatoes and serve.

New Potatoes with Gremolata

Easy Entertaining

Cooked in paper parcels with fresh herbs and the delicious tang of lemons this potato dish is full of flavour. Greaseproof paper can also be used but it is not as strong as baking parchment so use double thickness.

Ingredients for 2

450g/1lb baby new potatoes
2 tbsp chopped fresh parsley
2 tbsp chopped fresh mint
1 tsp lemon zest
1 tsp capers, rinsed and
  chopped
1 tsp lemon juice
2 tbsp extra virgin olive oil
salt and freshly ground
  black pepper

Ingredients for 4

900g/2lb baby new potatoes
4 tbsp chopped fresh parsley
4 tbsp chopped fresh mint
1 tbsp lemon zest
1 tbsp capers, rinsed and
  chopped
1 tbsp lemon juice
4 tbsp extra virgin olive oil
salt and freshly ground
  black pepper

1 Preheat the oven to 190°C/375°F/gas mark 5. Wash the potatoes and divide them equally between 2 (4) large squares of non-stick baking parchment.

2 Combine all the remaining ingredients.

3 Spoon equally over the potatoes.

4 Fold up the paper to form parcels that completely enclose the potatoes.

5 Place on a baking sheet and bake for 40-45 minutes, or until the potatoes are tender. Serve in the paper.

Caramelised Potatoes

The caramel coating can be used on other root vegetables such as carrots, turnips or parsnips, but I prefer it most with potatoes.

Ingredients for 2

450g/1lb small potatoes, peeled
25g/1oz butter
25g/1oz light muscovado sugar
1 tbsp water
salt
chopped fresh parsley to garnish

Ingredients for 4

900g/2lb small potatoes, peeled
50g/2oz butter
50g/2oz light muscovado sugar
2 tbsp water
salt
chopped fresh parsley to garnish

1 Bring a pan of water to the boil and lightly salt. Add the potatoes and simmer for 12–15 minutes until almost tender. Drain

2 Heat the butter in a sauté pan and stir in the sugar. Stir until the sugar dissolves then boil until slightly syrupy. Take care not to let the mixture burn; it should be a golden brown colour.

3 Add the water, taking care as it may splutter.

4 Swirl the pan and add the potatoes. Cook gently for about 10 minutes, shaking the pan occasionally, until the potatoes are golden and tender when pierced with a skewer.

5 Transfer to a warm serving dish and allow to stand for 2–3 minutes before serving.

Saag Aloo

This is a favourite of mine, which I have to order whenever I go to an Indian restaurant. It is also very easy to make at home, so my potato cookbook would not be complete without it.

Ingredients for 2

- 1/4 tsp cumin seeds
- 1/4 tsp fennel seeds
- 1/4 tsp coriander seeds
- 2 tbsp ghee or sunflower oil
- 1 small onion, chopped
- 1 tbsp fresh ginger, chopped
- 1/2 green chilli, seeded if desired and chopped
- 1/4 tsp salt
- 1/2 tsp ground turmeric
- 2 tsp lemon juice
- about 75ml/2 1/2fl oz water
- 450g/1lb floury potatoes, peeled and cut into chunks
- 225g/8oz spinach, washed

Ingredients for 4

- 1/2 tsp cumin seeds
- 1/2 tsp fennel seeds
- 1/2 tsp coriander seeds
- 4 tbsp ghee or sunflower oil
- 1 onion, chopped
- 2 tbsp fresh ginger, chopped
- 1 green chilli, seeded if desired and chopped
- 1/2 tsp salt
- 1 tsp ground turmeric
- 1 tbsp lemon juice
- about 150ml/1/4pt water
- 900g/2lb small floury potatoes, peeled and cut into chunks
- 450g/1lb spinach, washed

1 Heat the seeds in a dry frying pan until they begin to pop. Pour into a pestle and mortar and grind coarsely.

2 Heat the ghee or oil in a large saucepan and add the onion, ginger and chilli. Fry for 3–4 minutes until the onion begins to soften.

3 Add the ground seeds, salt, turmeric and lemon juice. Stir in the potatoes and water. Bring to the boil, reduce the heat, cover and cook over a low heat for about 10 minutes until the potatoes are almost tender.

4 Stir in the spinach and cook for a further 5 minutes, until the spinach has wilted and the potatoes are completely tender. Stir frequently to prevent it burning on the bottom of the pan. The mixture should be quite dry.

Sweet Potatoes with Chilli and Lime

A tasty side dish that goes well with grilled chicken or fish.

Ingredients for 2

450g/1lb sweet potatoes
25g/1oz butter
grated zest ¼ lime
1 tbsp lime juice
1 tbsp light muscovado
  sugar
2 tsp sweet chilli sauce

Ingredients for 4

900g/2lb sweet potatoes
50g/2oz butter
grated zest ½ lime
2 tbsp lime juice
25g/1oz light muscovado
  sugar
1 tbsp sweet chilli sauce

1 Peel and slice the potatoes. Cook in a large pan of lightly salted, boiling water for 5 minutes until just tender.

2 Drain well.

3 Melt the butter in a large frying pan and stir in the lime zest, juice, sugar and chilli sauce. Stir until the sugar dissolves.

4 Add the sweet potatoes and toss over the heat for 5–10 minutes until the potatoes are soft, piping hot and lightly coated with the glaze.

breads and bakes

Easy Potato Bread

Freezer Friendly

The potato gives this bread a moist crumb and increases its keeping quality. Depending on how soft your mashed potato is, you may not need all the milk, so do not add it all to begin with. The bread will freeze for up to 3 months.

Ingredients for 2

450g/1lb strong white bread flour
7g/¼ oz sachet easy blend yeast
1 tsp salt
2 tbsp olive oil
350g/12oz cooked mashed potato
about 250ml/9fl oz lukewarm water

1 Preheat the oven to 230°C/450°F/gas mark 8.

2 Place the flour in a mixing bowl and stir in the yeast and salt.

3 Make a well in the centre and add the oil, potato and most of the water. Mix to a soft dough, adding the remaining water if required.

4 Turn out onto a floured surface and knead for 5 minutes. Put in as much energy as you can at this stage to really stretch the dough.

5 Shape the dough into a round or oblong loaf. Place on a lightly oiled baking sheet.

6 Cover loosely with oiled cling wrap and leave in a warm place until doubled in size – about 1 hour.

7 Bake in a preheated oven for 30 minutes until well risen and golden. The loaf will sound hollow when tapped on the bottom. Cool on a wire rack.

Sun-dried Tomato and Olive Rolls

Easy Entertaining

Perfect for dinner parties or to add interest to packed lunches.
You may not need all the liquid, so do not add it all to begin with.

Makes 8 rolls:

450g/1lb strong white bread flour
7g/¼ oz sachet easy-blend yeast
1 tsp salt
4 pieces sun-dried tomatoes in oil, chopped
25g/1oz pitted black olives, chopped
2 tbsp oil from the sun-dried tomatoes
350g/12oz cooked mashed potato
about 250ml/9fl oz lukewarm water

1 Preheat the oven to 230°C/450°F/gas mark 8.

2 Place the flour in a mixing bowl and stir in the yeast and salt.

3 Make a well in the centre and add the tomatoes, olives, oil, potato and most of the water. Mix to a soft dough, adding the remaining water if required.

4 Turn out onto a floured surface and knead for 5 minutes. Put in as much energy as you can at this stage to really stretch the dough.

5 Divide the dough into 8 and shape each piece into a ball. Place on a lightly oiled baking sheet.

6 Cover loosely with oiled cling wrap and leave in a warm place until doubled in size about 1 hour.

7 Bake in a preheated oven for about 20 minutes until well risen and golden. The rolls will sound hollow when tapped on the bottom. Cool on a wire rack.

Pizza Con Le Patate

vegetarian

I first tried this style of pizza on holiday in Rome many years ago. It has remained a firm favourite and makes a great light supper dish or an alternative to a lunchtime sandwich. Its often made with rosemary but I rather like it with thyme.

Ingredients for 2

225g/8oz strong plain flour
1/4 tsp salt
1/2 tsp easy blend yeast
extra virgin olive oil
about 175ml/6fl oz lukewarm
　　water
400g/14oz waxy potatoes,
　　peeled
1 onion, sliced
1 tbsp thyme leaves
2 cloves garlic, chopped
fresh thyme to garnish

Ingredients for 4

450g/1lb strong plain flour
1/2 tsp salt
1 tsp easy blend yeast
extra virgin olive oil
about 350ml/12fl oz
　　lukewarm water
800g/1lb 12oz waxy potatoes,
　　peeled
2 onions, sliced
2 tbsp thyme leaves
4 cloves garlic, chopped
fresh thyme to garnish

1　Sift the flour and salt into a bowl, stir in the yeast. Add 1 tbsp (2tbsp) olive oil and enough warm water to mix to a soft dough – knead it lightly.

2　Roll out the dough to 1 (2) rectangle(s), about 30 x 20cm/12 x 8in. Fold over a small border, pinching the dough in place, to form a raised edge.

3　Cover with oiled cling wrap and leave in a warm place for about 30 minutes until it begins to rise .

4　Preheat the oven to 220°C/425°F/gas mark 7. Boil the potatoes for 5 minutes, drain and slice. Toss in thyme, garlic and a little olive oil.

5　Arrange the onions over the pizza base with the potato slices on top.

6　Bake for 15 minutes then reduce the heat to 190°C/375°F/gas mark 5 and continue to cook for about 25 minutes until golden. Serve cut into pieces, garnished with fresh thyme.

Salami and Red Onion Pizza

Family Favourite

Pizza is always popular in our household and this pizza base is quicker to make than the more traditional bread base.

Ingredients for 2

175g/6oz self-raising flour
pinch salt
75g/3oz cold mashed potato
2 tbsp olive oil
about 75ml2¹/₂fl oz milk
2 tbsp tomato pizza topping
    or tomato purée
1 small red onion, peeled
    and cut into thin wedges
25g/1oz salami, cut into
    strips
60g/2¹/₂oz mozzarella cheese,
    sliced
basil leaves to garnish

Ingredients for 4

350g/12oz self-raising flour
pinch salt
175g/6oz cold mashed potato
3 tbsp olive oil
about 150ml/¹/₄pt milk
4 tbsp tomato pizza topping
    or tomato purée
2 small red onions, peeled
    and cut into thin wedges
50g/2oz salami, cut into
    strips
150g/5oz mozzarella cheese,
    sliced
basil leaves to garnish

1 Preheat the oven to 200°C/400°F/gas mark 6. Sift the flour and salt into a bowl.

2 Add the potato, 1 tbsp (2tbsp) oil, and enough milk to mix to a soft dough (you may not need all the milk).

3 Roll out to form 1 (2) 23cm/9in pizza base(s) and place on a lightly greased baking sheet.

4 Spread the tomato topping or purée over the pizza base. Heat the remaining oil and lightly sauté the onions until just beginning to soften. Arrange on the pizza.

5 Scatter the salami over the top and lay the cheese on top. Bake for 25–30 minutes until the base is cooked and golden and the cheese is melted and beginning to brown. Garnish with basil.

Salami and Red Onion Pizza

Family Favourite

Pizza is always popular in our household and this pizza base is quicker to make than the more traditional bread base.

Ingredients for 2

175g/6oz self-raising flour
pinch salt
75g/3oz cold mashed potato
2 tbsp olive oil
about 75ml2¹/₂fl oz milk
2 tbsp tomato pizza topping
   or tomato purée
1 small red onion, peeled
   and cut into thin wedges
25g/1oz salami, cut into
   strips
60g/2¹/₂oz mozzarella cheese,
   sliced
basil leaves to garnish

Ingredients for 4

350g/12oz self-raising flour
pinch salt
175g/6oz cold mashed potato
3 tbsp olive oil
about 150ml/¹/₄pt milk
4 tbsp tomato pizza topping
   or tomato purée
2 small red onions, peeled
   and cut into thin wedges
50g/2oz salami, cut into
   strips
150g/5oz mozzarella cheese,
   sliced
basil leaves to garnish

1 Preheat the oven to 200°C/400°F/gas mark 6. Sift the flour and salt into a bowl.

2 Add the potato, 1 tbsp (2tbsp) oil, and enough milk to mix to a soft dough (you may not need all the milk).

3 Roll out to form 1 (2) 23cm/9in pizza base(s) and place on a lightly greased baking sheet.

4 Spread the tomato topping or purée over the pizza base. Heat the remaining oil and lightly sauté the onions until just beginning to soften. Arrange on the pizza.

5 Scatter the salami over the top and lay the cheese on top. Bake for 25–30 minutes until the base is cooked and golden and the cheese is melted and beginning to brown. Garnish with basil.

Spicy Beef and Potato Crescents

These pastry bites are great for parties. I have given the quantity for a smaller amount but they can be frozen uncooked and thawed when required.

Ingredients for 2

1 tbsp olive oil
1/2 small onion, chopped
1 clove garlic, chopped
1/2 chilli, seeded and
    chopped
100g/4oz potato, peeled and
    diced
75g/3oz lean mince beef
1/4 tsp each cumin, coriander
    and turmeric
75ml/21/2fl oz water
225g/8oz shortcrust pastry
beaten egg to glaze

Ingredients for 4

2 tbsp olive oil
1 small onion, chopped
2 cloves garlic, chopped
1 chilli, seeded and chopped
200g/7oz potato, peeled and
    diced
175g/6oz lean mince beef
1/2 tsp each cumin, coriander
    and turmeric
150ml/1/4pt water
450g/1lb shortcrust pastry
beaten egg to glaze

1 Heat the oil in a frying pan and sauté the onion and garlic for 3–4 minutes until softened.

2 Add the chilli and potato and sauté for 5 minutes, turning frequently.

3 Add the meat and cook until browned, breaking up with a spoon as it cooks. Add the spices and water.

4 Simmer for 20 minutes until the potato is tender and the liquid has evaporated.

5 Roll the pastry on a lightly floured work surface and cut out 7.5cm/3in circles.

6 Pile a little of the meat filling into each centre. Fold over the pastry and pinch edges together to seal. Repeat until all the pastry and filling is used.

7 Brush with beaten egg. Bake in a preheated oven 200°C/400°F/gas mark 6 for 15–20 minutes until golden.

Chicken and Potato Pie

Family Favourite

I find meat pies work best if the pastry is only on the top. The potato gives the pastry a fabulous crumbly texture. A food processor makes this a very easy pastry to make. If you do not have one, you can mix all the pastry ingredients together with a fork. It takes a little more effort but it is just as successful.

Ingredients for 2

Pastry:

50g/2oz cold mashed potato
100g/4oz plain flour
50g/2oz butter, softened
beaten egg to glaze

Filling:

25g/1oz butter
75g/3oz mushrooms, sliced
1 small leek, sliced
25g/1oz plain flour
150ml/¹/₄pt chicken stock
75ml/2¹/₂fl oz milk
225g/8oz cooked chicken
salt and freshly ground
**   black pepper**

Ingredients for 4

Pastry:

100g/4oz cold mashed potato
225g/8oz plain flour
100g/4oz butter, softened
beaten egg to glaze

Filling:

50g/2oz butter
175g/6oz mushrooms, sliced
1 large leek, sliced
50g/2oz plain flour
300ml/¹/₂pt chicken stock
150ml/¹/₄pt milk
450g/1lb cooked chicken
salt and freshly ground
**   black pepper**

1 Place all the ingredients for the pastry in a food processor and process until combined to form a soft dough. Chill.

2 Preheat the oven to 200°C/400°F/gas mark 6.

3 To make the filling, melt the butter in a small pan and sauté the mushrooms and leek for about 5 minutes until softened.

4 Stir in the flour and cook for a few seconds. Gradually stir in the stock and milk. Cook gently, stirring, until the sauce thickens. Add the chicken. Season with mustard, salt and pepper.

5 Roll out a little of the pastry and cut a thin strip that will fit the edge of one pie dish or small individual pie dishes. Dampen the pie dish with a little beaten egg and stick the pastry in place.

6 Pour the chicken mixture into the pie dish.

7 Roll out the remaining pastry to cover the dish. Dampen the pastry strip and place the pastry lid on top. Press edges down with a fork to seal.

8 Cut a small slit in the pastry to allow the steam to escape and decorate with pie trimming if desired. Brush with a little beaten egg.

9 Bake for 30–40 minutes until pastry is crisp and golden.

Cheese and Potato Pasties

Freezer Friendly

These are ideal for picnics and packed lunches.

Ingredients for 2

225g/8oz plain flour
100g/4oz butter
1 to 2 tbsp water
1 tbsp olive oil
1 small onion, chopped
175g/6oz sweet potatoes, peeled and diced
175g/6oz potatoes, peeled and diced
100g/4oz Cheshire cheese, diced
beaten egg to glaze
salt and freshly ground black pepper

Ingredients for 4

450g/1lb plain flour
225g/8oz butter
3 to 4 tbsp water
2 tbsp olive oil
1 large onion, chopped
350g/12oz sweet potatoes, peeled and diced
350g/12oz potatoes, peeled and diced
225g/8oz Cheshire cheese, diced
beaten egg to glaze
salt and freshly ground black pepper

1 Place the flour in a mixing bowl and rub the butter into the flour until the mixture resembles fine breadcrumbs. Add enough water to mix to make a firm dough. Chill while preparing the filling.

2 Heat the oil in a small pan and fry the onion until soft.

3 Cook the potato for 5 minutes and the sweet potatoes for 3 minutes in lightly salted boiling water until just tender. Allow to cool.

4 Combine the onion, potato and cheese and season with a little pepper. Preheat the oven to 200°C/400°F/gas mark 6. Lightly grease a baking sheet.

5 Roll out the pastry on a lightly floured work surface and cut out 4 (8) 18cm/7in circles using a tea plate as a guide.

6 Divide the potato mixture between the circles, brush the edges with beaten egg and fold over to enclose the filling.

7 Pinch the edges together to seal. Cut a small hole in each to allow the steam to escape.

8 Place on the prepared baking sheet and brush with beaten egg. Bake in the centre of the oven for 30 minutes or until golden.

Savoury Potato Scones with Cheese and Chives

Serve these yummy savoury scones as part of a packed lunch or with a meal in place of bread.

Ingredients for 2

25g/1oz butter
75g/3oz self-raising flour
50g/2oz Cheshire cheese,
   grated
1 tbsp snipped fresh chives
100g/4oz cold mashed potato
1 to 2 tbsp milk, plus extra
   for brushing

Ingredients for 4

50g/2oz butter
175g/6oz self-raising flour
100g/4 oz Cheshire cheese,
   grated
2 tbsp snipped fresh chives
225g/8oz cold mashed potato
2 to 3 tbsp milk plus extra for
   brushing

1 Preheat oven to 200°C/400°F/gas mark 6.

2 Rub the butter into the flour, until the mixture resembles fine breadcrumbs.

3 Stir in most of the cheese and chives. Add the mashed potato and mix well. Add enough milk to bring the mixture together to form a soft dough.

4 Roll out the dough to about 2cm/3/4in thick and cut out 7.5cm/3in scones using a round cookie cutter. Place on a lightly greased baking sheet.

5 Brush the tops with a little extra milk and sprinkle the remaining cheese on top. Bake for 20 minutes or until risen and golden. Serve warm.

Potato Griddle Scones

Adding potato to scones gives a light moist texture that is absolutely delicious. I love baking scones on a griddle as I find that they have a great flavour and it fills the house with a fantastic aroma.

Ingredients for 2

75g/3oz self-raising flour
¼ tsp baking powder
25g/1oz butter
25g/1oz caster sugar
40g/1½oz sultanas (optional)
100g/4oz cold mashed potato
a little milk

Ingredients for 4

175g/6oz self-raising flour
½ tsp baking powder
50g/2oz butter
50g/2oz caster sugar
75g/3oz sultanas (optional)
225g/8oz cold mashed potato
a little milk

1 Sift the flour and baking powder into a bowl. Rub in the butter, until the mixture resembles fine breadcrumbs.

2 Stir in the sugar and sultanas, if using. Add the mashed potato and mix well.

3 Add enough milk to bring the mixture together to form a soft dough. The amount of milk required will depend on how soft the mash is; you may not need any.

4 Shape into a flat round about 2cm/¾in thick.

5 Heat a flat griddle pan or heavy-based frying pan until hot. Lightly oil the griddle, place the scone on it and cook for 6–8 minutes each side over a low heat until golden and crisp.

6 Serve warm or cold, cut into wedges and spread with butter or jam, if desired.

Sweet Potato Pie

A classic American flan with a creamy, moist filling, this is best served warm, either on its own, with whipped cream or with my preferred choice crème fraîche.

Ingredients for 8 to 10:

350g/12oz shortcrust pastry
900g/2lb sweet potatoes
50g/2oz butter
5 eggs
175g/6oz light muscovado sugar
200g/7oz can evaporated milk
1 tbsp lemon juice
1 tsp vanilla essence
1½ tsp mixed spice

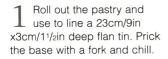

1 Roll out the pastry and use to line a 23cm/9in x3cm/1½in deep flan tin. Prick the base with a fork and chill.

2 Peel and cut the potatoes into chunks. Steam or boil for 15 minutes until just tender. Drain and purée in a food processor. Add the butter and whizz to blend.

3 Preheat the oven to 200°C/400°F/gas mark 6. Line the pastry case with greaseproof paper and baking beans and bake for 10 minutes. Remove the paper and beans and bake for 10 minutes.

4 Reduce the oven temperature to 170°C/325°F/gas mark 3.

5 Whisk the eggs and sugar together until well combined. Beat in the sweet potato purée, milk, lemon juice, vanilla and spice.

6 Pour into the pastry case and bake for 20 minutes, or until the filling is just set. Allow to cool slightly before serving.

Apple and Chocolate Upside Down Cakes

Freezer Friendly

These individual puddings are very moist and make a great midweek treat. They can be frozen for up to 2 months. Defrost completely and serve cold or warmed through in the oven to serve.

Ingredients for 10:

about 4 tbsp golden syrup
2 small apples
100g/4oz butter, softened
100g/4oz caster sugar
100g/4oz cold mashed potatoes
2 eggs, lightly beaten
2 tbsp milk
100g/4oz self-raising flour
2 tbsp cocoa powder

1 Preheat the oven to 180°C/350°F/gas mark 4. Lightly grease 10 muffin cups.

2 Place a generous teaspoon of golden syrup into each muffin cup. Core and slice the apples and arrange a few slices in the bottom of each cup on top of the syrup.

3 Beat together the butter and sugar until pale and fluffy. Beat in the potatoes. Gradually beat in the eggs. Stir in the milk.

4 Sift the flour and cocoa powder together and carefully fold into the sponge mixture. Divide the mixture equally between the cups.

5 Bake for 25 minutes. Allow to cool in the tin for 5 minutes before turning out onto a tray. Serve with cream or custard.

Ginger Bread Fingers

Low Fat

Not too sweet, these ginger cake fingers are fabulous served with a cup of coffee.

Ingredients for 18 fingers:

275g/10oz self-raising flour
2 tsp bicarbonate of soda
2 tsp ground ginger
1 tsp mixed spice
175g/6oz floury potatoes, peeled and grated
75g/3oz stem ginger, chopped
100g/4oz golden syrup
100g/4oz black treacle
100ml/3¹/₂fl oz sunflower oil
2 eggs, lightly beaten
2 tbsp water

1 Preheat the oven to 180°C/350°F/gas mark 4. Lightly grease and line the base of a 20 x 25cm/8 x 10in cake tin.

2 Sift the flour, soda and spices into a mixing bowl.

3 Stir in the potatoes and stem ginger.

4 Heat the syrup, treacle and oil together in a small pan, stirring until combined.

5 Stir into the flour mixture, along with the egg and water. Beat until well combined.

6 Pour into the prepared tin and bake for 30 minutes. Allow to cool in the tin for 5 minutes before turning out onto a wire rack to cool completely. Serve cut into 18 fingers.

Jam Pudding

Family Favourite

Adding potatoes to sweet dishes may seem a little strange but they actually help to give a moist texture and improve the keeping qualities. If preferred, you can use golden syrup in place of the jam. If you have a microwave, use it to cook the pudding and it will be ready in minutes.

Ingredients for 6:

100g/4oz butter, softened
100g/4oz caster sugar
100g/4oz cold mashed potatoes
2 tbsp milk
2 eggs, lightly beaten
100g/4oz self-raising flour
4 tbsp jam of your choice

1 Beat together the butter and sugar until pale and fluffy and then beat in the potatoes. Gradually beat in the milk and eggs.

2 Fold in the flour until just combined.

3 Lightly grease a 1.2l/2pt pudding basin. Spoon the jam into the base.

4 Carefully pour the cake batter over the jam. Cover securely with greaseproof paper or foil and steam for 1¹/₂ hours. Allow to cool in the bowl for 10 minutes, before turning out onto a serving plate.

5 Alternately, cook in the microwave. Cover the bowl with cling wrap, leaving a space for the steam to escape. Microwave on full power (850W) for 4 minutes. The surface of the cake should be almost completely dry with just a small damp area. Allow to stand for 5 minutes before turning out.

index

credits & acknowledgements

Thanks to all those friends and family members who gave suggestions as to their favourite potato recipes. Especially, thanks to my fantastic father-in-law, Richard, for his constant encouragement.

Thanks to Premier Cutlery (www.premiercutlery.co.uk.) for supplying the knives and some of the small kitchen utensils used for the step-by-step pictures. Also thanks to Magimix whose food processor has well and truly earned its place on my kitchen worktop and whose deep-fat fryer has safely fried more than the odd potato or two.

I would like to thank Colin Bowling and Paul Forrester for their creative photography and their tasting notes.